The Lord *of* Glory

The Transforming Presence

of Jesus Christ

Chris Strevel

Scripture quotations are from the King James Version
Cover Design by:
Bill Higgins - gallerycreativeinc.com
Waves photograph: Tobias Van Schneider - Unsplash.com

To the Reader

"That I may know him" (Phil. 3:10). Few have known him better than the Apostle Paul. The more he knew him, the more he wanted to know him. The Savior of the world is fairer than ten thousand, full of grace and truth. Grace to grace, glory to glory – this is the flow of life and love in the kingdom of Jesus Christ. "Let him kiss me with the kisses of his mouth" – this is the believer's deepest longing (Song of Songs 1:2). Let me know more of his love, his interceding power, his calming sovereignty, his indwelling peace. Let him cleanse me, renew and sanctify me, and lead me in the paths of righteousness. Never can we exhaust his riches or the glory of his person and work, become too obsessed with him, or outlive our need of him.

Too many of his friends think of him primarily in the past or future tense – his cross and second coming. Little do they think of him in the present tense, his abiding life in us today, his constant intercession for us at the Father's right hand, and his ruling over all things for the sake of his Church. Jesus Christ is the only reality, the only life, the only truth. He was dead, but he is alive forever. He is Christ in us, the hope of glory. Our lives are wrapped up with his life. We are waiting for a banquet of love, the return of the King, our glory in the Lord of glory.

It is my belief that the failure in my life, and perhaps in yours, to be captivated by the glory of Jesus Christ is our greatest weakness. There is no life anywhere but in union with Jesus Christ. As we learn of him, he unfolds his abundant life in us. Our problems and sorrows find their solution here – "That they may behold my glory" (John 17:24). "But we all, beholding as in a glass the glory of the Lord, are changed into the same image, from glory to glory, even by the Spirit of the Lord" (2 Cor. 3:18). Jesus' glory is transforming as we draw near to him in faith and fellowship. We must stretch our minds and hearts to behold by faith his glory now (2 Cor. 4:18).

Our exalted Savior has lost none of his freshness, power, and relevance in the modern world. Much of what we call modern, with all of its social, civil, domestic, and personal upheaval, is the fruit of turning from his glory and embracing emptiness. He has not spared his church from the confusion of our times. Whenever the glory of his person and work grows dim and experiential religion loses its central place in God's church, Ichabod is in danger of being written over our doors. Only holding fast to Christ and his glory makes us steadfast in holding fast to his eternal truth. Glory or no glory. Jesus Christ or vanity. Jesus Christ or personal emptiness. Jesus Christ or political tyranny. As you read, pray more earnestly than Moses did on Sinai, for we have freer and fuller access than he did, "Lord, show me your glory" (Exodus 33:18). He will, for he has promised. We have beheld his glory. The glory now dwells with us, and we with him. Beholding his glory is his prayer for us. It is the only strength unto holiness. It is our destiny.

These essays are grouped by themes related to the person and work of Jesus Christ. One reason for their apparent and likely disjointedness is that they were written over a period of many years, included as a bulletin insert for the edification of my beloved congregation. They were stand-alone essays that I have called "From the Pastor's Desk." Perhaps a better title would be "The glory of Jesus Christ confronting and changing your pastor." With all believers, I need his continual renewal, to see the glory of God in his face, and to be transformed by his glory. Despite their deficiencies, I have been encouraged to make the effort to compile and publish them in one place. If they encourage you to seek Jesus Christ and to see his glory a little more clearly, I will rejoice greatly in God my Savior. May the Lord of Glory transform us more and more into his image!

Table of Contents

~1~
Glory Incarnate

Who Is This?

After a full day of preaching and ministering to lost souls, Jesus and his disciples boarded a boat at Capernaum to make a night crossing of the Sea of Tiberias. In the midst of the passage, a tempest arose, with peals of thunder and bolts of lightning. Threatening a watery grave, the turbulent wind pushed the sea into the small vessel. Panic stricken, the disciples searched the boat for Jesus. They found him asleep, weary from his work, gathering strength for the day ahead, unmindful of the howling wind and perilous storm surge. The disciples awakened him with shouts, pleading with him to act, to save them. Hearing their yells above the din and seeing their horror-stricken faces, he stood up, rebuked the wind and waves, saying, "Peace, be still." Calm. Silence. The sudden and gentle lapping of the tide against the boat. The sheer terror on their faces gave way to utter bewilderment. Who is this? He looked at them and asked: "Why are you so fearful, O you of little faith" (Mark 4:40).

The disciples feared the storm outside the boat. They should have feared the One with them in the boat. In their time with Jesus, they had seen miracles and heard marvelous words. They believed Jesus to be the promised Messiah. They were beginners, however, at knowing him in his glory and power. They did not realize that he who made the seas could calm them with a word. He sat above the floods, above the chaos of life, entering into it, yes, for our sakes, yet never in danger of being capsized by the turbulence. The wind and the seas obey him.

He is Lord, not simply in the sense of a religious figure to whom we must give allegiance as our ancient, venerated Master or as unto a power beyond our understanding. He is Lord personally, absolutely, and historically. Everything obeys him, even things far beyond our control or understanding. Whatever is happening around us, however horrible those events may be, he sits as King above the flood. He is accomplishing his holy and wise purposes. He uses the chaos of life to draw us before his throne of grace, where we find calm, strength, and wisdom.

Who Is This?

The child of God has only one legitimate fear. The Bible says that the Lord is our fear, our dread (Isa. 8:13). This fear is not the superstitious anxiety of the heathen, whether backward tribesmen or ancient Greek bards. We are not to fear God because he might suddenly send a lightning bolt upon us if we do evil or arouse the forces of nature against us if we displease him. No, we fear him because we stand in holy awe of him, of his majesty and greatness, of his holiness and penetrating gaze, of his power and strength, of his love and grace. We fear him because he is not capricious, but just, not arbitrary, but ever consistent with himself. We fear him because our hearts are drawn by his Spirit to love him for who he is. It is a curious combination. The Lord and God whom we fear so deeply is also the One we love so ardently. True love for him is built upon awe and wonder. Unless we know something of his greatness, we cannot truly love him and will never give ourselves completely to him.

If we fear God, we need fear nothing else. Take, for example, the Proverb: "Be not afraid of sudden terror, neither of the desolation of the wicked when it comes. For the Lord will be your confidence and keep your foot from being taken" (3:25-26). Believers often find themselves living in very turbulent times. Through them, the Lord shows us that our safe ships are not quite so safe after all. The Lord confronts us with storm, with peril. And when the storm is more widespread, as when unbelieving men and nations are judged for their rebellion through events that only a blind man would not attribute to the hand of God, we are caught up in them. Finding ourselves surrounded by fearful men proclaiming the end of the world, we feel that the waves of life threaten our destruction. We run around like half-crazed men, unhinged by fear, sensing disaster but feeling powerless to do anything about it. One says, "Do this." Another says, "You must do this to survive the coming storm." All the while, the Lord of glory is with us. Even if he seems to be sleeping, a word from him is sufficient. A question from him exposes our idolatry, that we fear the wrong things: loss of health, prosperity, position, or even life.

We should expect guilty men to proclaim the end of the world whenever their world begins to collapse. Whatever unbelieving man says about himself, God says that he is "like the waves of the sea, driven and tossed by the wind." He may be quite sophisticated, well-educated, or wealthy. Nevertheless, he has no rest. He is cut off from his God and alienated in his mind through wicked works. Since the Lord made us for himself, there can be no inner peace, no lasting security for the man that seeks life apart from God. His guilt is constant. He may not be able to define his haunting fear; he may even deny its existence. Yet, man is who God says he is, not who man says he is.

A sense of alienation from God is often marked by an "end of the world" mentality, a paralyzing spiral of unbelief that we see everywhere operative in the West, from climate to currency. The decisions made to avoid the feared peril actually intensify it. These efforts are man's foolish attempt to protect himself from the God whom he fears but to whom he will not yield. Thus, when his world of armies and bureaucracies, his efforts at manipulation and control begin to collapse, when his hubris is confronted by the reality of God's providence and justice, of course it will seem to him that the whole world is ending with him. He wants others to be fearful, for this justifies his own fears. It also gives him the opportunity to control others through fear, for fear is one of the greatest control mechanisms Satan ever invented.

The desolation of the wicked will come. His entire worldview is a huge ponzi scheme to escape the claims of the living God, enslave others while amassing personal wealth, and insulate himself from the general havoc his rebellion always creates. Solomon assumes, as all the Bible does, that the desolation of the wicked will come. It rarely comes when and how we think it will, for our Father is merciful and longsuffering. He gives men time to repent. He gives his church time to proclaim the gospel to his elect in the four corners of the land. For the sake of his Church, for whose sake he has given his Son dominion over all things, he might even forestall the judgment, giving us time to repent, see his hand working, and take refuge in him. But the judgment will come. Over six thousand years of world history is strewn with the rotting corpses and decaying civilizations that sought to build their own towers of Babel, large and small, arrogant empire and separatist enclave, all gone.

We are not to fear this desolation. We are to expect it and the furious storms it creates. Remember, these are the Lord's storms, outbreaks of his displeasure against the world of ungodly men, historical reminders that there is another King, anticipations of the final judgment. God's desolating work against the city of man can be quite devastating. Since we live in God's world, even as his precious sheep, we will see and feel the tremors of his wrath. He sends them to awaken us from our stupor and to stir us up to seek him. Like the disciples in the boat, we must run to Jesus when the storms of life mount, when the wicked stir up mire and dirt, when their rebellion crashes upon the crags of God's providence and purposes – and the throne of his Son.

Whenever these storms arise, we immediately begin rowing harder in the boat, doing all within our limited means and ability to preserve ourselves. Since fearing God means recognizing these storms as his work, we should make adequate preparation. Whatever providential manifestation of God's displeasure a particular age of man experiences, those with eyes to see should wake up, take notice, and adjust their lives accordingly. If God is judging materialism, we should repent of our covetousness. If he is judging immorality, we must seek purity of heart and life in him. If the Lord is toppling financial markets, we should put our own financial houses in order and live within our means. There is only so much we can do, especially when God's judgments are widespread.

In seasons of general upheaval, I often think of pious Israelite families like Daniel's, who watched their son being carted away as a captive to serve a foreign court. They were undoubtedly leading godly lives, for Daniel's convictions did not arise out of thin air once he arrived in Babylon. Though Daniel's parents could not have known it at the time, their gut-wrenching loss was the very means God used to diffuse his glory in a larger sphere, through the piety and faithfulness of one committed man. Daniel's life reminds us that even something as horrible as the radical displacement and separation of families is always purposeful. When we are tempted to fight back, to go out shooting, so to speak, we would do well to remember this.

Thankfully, Daniel's parents were not of this mentality, choosing to die together in some sort of Alamo last stand rather than submit to the Lord's greater providences, which they could neither see nor understand. All our storm preparations, then, which are good and necessary, must never ignore the fact that our human means are always secondary to God's larger purposes. Use them, but do not trust them. God may use them; then again, he may simply bypass them to accomplish his wonderful purposes for us. The very reason the Lord brings the storms is to draw us away from every other confidence and teach us to run to him.

When the storms come, let us not run around in our little boats as the disciples did, as fear-crazed men, knowing yet not knowing who was with them in the boat. We know who he is. He is the Lord of glory. All things have been given into his hand. His sole purpose in bringing the desolation of the wicked is to revive, reform, and restore his Church. We need him to topple our idols; he will. We need him to test and purify our faith; he will. We need him to work so gloriously as to set our affections more firmly on his eternal kingdom; he will. We need him to draw a clearer line of demarcation between his Church and the world; he will. We need him to make us more mindful of our citizenship in heaven; he will. We need him to make us holy; he will. He does all these things as the crucified and risen Lord of heaven and earth, the Savior and Shepherd of his people and the Judge of the nations. Finding us asleep, he stirs up the storms of life to lead us to seek refuge, comfort, and life in him. Amid the unnerving din of his providences, wake up, believer, and hear his calm and challenging call to you: "Why are you so fearful? It is I, be not afraid."

And the Word Became Flesh

Because the Lord has given us much to do, we need seasons of quiet. Quiet is at the heart of strength, for it allows for communion with God (Isa. 30:15). His majesty, words, love, and fellowship call for quiet stillness before him. Noisy lives and noisy souls tend to push him away, drown out his still, small voice. He says "be still and know that I am God" (Ps. 46:1). If we would know him, we must be still.

Certain Scriptures require more believing, seeking stillness than others. Consider John 1:14: "And the word was made flesh, and dwelt among us, (and we beheld his glory; the glory as of the only begotten of the Father,) full of grace and truth." It is at the heart of our faith. Everything good and noble for our race, all peace and prosperity for the nations, and, most importantly, our deliverance from sin's curse and our restoration to God's favor depend upon its truth. What we believe about this verse is the difference between heresy and orthodoxy, being part of a cult or standing in the pure river of revealed religion.

By "Word," John does not mean a force or an idea. He does not mean God's thinking and reasoning, as if word is to be equated with the logic of the divine mind. The Word is the One about whom he has been speaking in the previous thirteen verses. The name "Word" indicates that he is the revelation of God. Only he who came forth from God as God can reveal God (1:18). If we would know God as our Father, we must hear the Son as the eternal Word of God (Luke 9:35). To deny or to break this chain cuts off man from knowledge, from redemption, and from God.

"In the beginning" (v. 1) is an absolute phrase that strikingly parallels Genesis 1:1 and is equivalent to "before there was anything else." When there was nothing but God, perfectly sufficient and contented in himself, there was also the Word. This excludes the Word from the rank of creature. As John immediately adds, "The Word was with God, and the Word was God." There is thus a distinction of persons within the essence of the one God. To the shema of Israel stressing God's unity (Deut. 6:4) must be added the Word of God stressing his personal diversity.

The Word is not a lesser person than God, for he is the person through whom "All things were made" (v. 2). The Word is not created; he is the Creator. Creatures by definition are not creators. Creatures draw their life and inspiration from another. He who made the worlds drew his life from himself. This is the reason John adds that "in him was life" (v. 4): absolutely, as the divine origin of all life. In every conceivable way, the Holy Spirit teaches us that this Word is the Creator-God, one with and distinct from the Father, eternal, having all life and glory in himself. All creatures draw their life from the eternal Word.

This very Word "became flesh." Here we encounter glory that set the angels to singing. At no other time than the incarnation of the Word did the angelic hosts become visible as a group to men and fill the earth with their holy praise. They did when the Word was born of woman. "Became" cannot possibly mean that God turned into man, the Creator into a creature. This is a revealed impossibility. So immeasurably higher and different are God's ways and thoughts from ours (Isa. 55:8-9) that the thought of the eternal God turning into a creature is repulsive in the extreme. To affirm such is to affirm the possibility of man's divinization or perfectibility, which is a thoroughly pagan, utopian, and statist ideal. "Became flesh" means that to his divine nature the eternal Word added a true and complete human nature. He "took upon himself the form of a servant. He humbled himself in order to redeem us; he "was made in the likeness of men" (Phil. 2:6-8).

By becoming flesh, the Word did not cease being God. John adds that "we beheld his glory, the glory as of the only begotten of the Father." "As of" does not mean a comparative glory, as a mirror might reflect the light of the sun, but the incarnate Word manifested his divine and eternal glory, the very glory that he shared with the Father from the foundation of the world (John 17:5). Granted, this was veiled under the lowliness of his humiliation (Phil. 2:6-7), but the disciples nonetheless beheld its mediated rays in his words and works. The purpose of "as of" is not to create distance between the glory of the Father and the glory of the incarnate Word but to identify them as closely as possible.

This is further supported by the phrase, "Only begotten of the Father," which means "uniquely begotten" or "one of a kind begotten." This further removes the glory of the Word from anything creaturely. What the apostles heard when he spoke and saw when he worked led them to believe nothing less than that he was "My Lord and my God" (John 20:28). They confessed that he was the Son of God – not a son in the way believers are, not a lesser deity, not simply a glimmer of glory, but the very glory of God revealed in human flesh (Matt. 16:16; John 6:68-69). The glory of the Word incarnate was an eternal, non-created, non-derived, glory. He is Emmanuel, God with us.

These details are important. Jesus Christ will never grip our souls or be more to us than a religious symbol, icon, or sentimental favorite unless we see something of who he truly was. Consider our struggle with sin. This terminal disease has stalked us since the moment of our conception. Over time, we accept its particular manifestations in our lives and grow comfortable with them. The "Word became flesh" should make us uncomfortable, for he assumed our nature to enter fully into our struggle against sin, overcome sin by his obedience, and provide atonement for sin through his sufferings. Therefore, we cannot simply live with our sins. We must look to the Word. His incarnation declares war against sin. His royal sympathy gives us encouragement to resist. His death, resurrection, and intercession at God's right hand assure redemption and newness of life. The Word became Flesh to overcome sin and destroy the works of the devil (1 John 3:8). In him, we are called to overcome sin and resist the devil. He will flee (James 4:7).

When the Word became flesh, he affirmed our earthly, physical life. Life on earth, life in the body matters. The way we conduct our business, run our homes, and relate to other flesh-and-blood creatures matters. The Christian faith is earthy. Yes, we long to "depart and be with Christ" and "look for the eternal city that hath foundations," but the way to these joys is through earthly faithfulness, get-your- hands- dirty diligence and service. It does no good to speak of "principles" and "walking by faith" unless these are lived out in daily, breathing, tangible love for God and man through obedience. The "Word became flesh" shows us that our problem is not flesh and blood but sin.

As for the eternal realities for which we long, our ultimate hope is not a disembodied existence, for again, the "Word became flesh." He remains so, ascended and glorified to be sure, but very much the incarnate Word. Why else will he raise our bodies from the dust but so that we may be whole again, the way God intended? The centrality of bodily resurrection to the Christian hope bears witness that the future state will be in some sense tangible. We know little about it now, and it certainly challenges our understanding and expectations of the nature of reality. Yet it will be a city, kingdom, and eternity for flesh-and-blood creatures – changed, immortal, and incorruptible, but flesh and blood nonetheless.

Because the Word became flesh, all tyrants over the realm of flesh must submit to his reign. The "must" is a historical and divine necessity; they will submit to him or be crushed. Having laid down his life for us and taken it up again, the Son of Man has taken up the mediatorial kingdom promised to him (Ps. 2:7-12; Dan. 7:13-14). He is now the King of every earthly king, the Prince of the kings of the earth (1 Tim. 6:15; Rev. 1:5). In his mediatorial person, he alone unites heaven and earth, God and man. Therefore, statism is a doomed enterprise. Tyranny has a short life-cycle. Governments may overstep their bounds and seek to dominate all things. Police may militarize and bully men for the slightest infraction. Corporations may get their hands dirty fomenting and profiting from wars. The kings and great ones of the earth plot, scheme, and imagine vain things (Ps. 2:1-3). Behind them lies Satan, plotting and scheming against the God-man King whom he cannot now touch (Rev. 12:17). Because the Word became flesh, the flow of history is "death to all tyrants." This will come at his hand. Jesus Christ is the only Lord of heaven and earth. All other claims to such monolithic power, whether it is the silly globalism so coveted by the elites or more local expressions of tyranny, will be put down. There is another King, one Jesus. Every knee must bow to him or face his wrath.

And the Word Became Flesh

When we are afflicted by the King's enemies, when they try to gobble up everything by their taxes, suffocating legislation, and wars, we have recourse on earth to heaven. Heaven has already invaded fallen earth and won. It is our responsibility to call upon the enthroned King, our Lord Jesus, asking him to thrust in his gospel sickle and to reap what he has been promised. If we are faithful where he has called us to serve him, we shall share in his victory. The only inevitability of history is that Jesus Christ, not man, is King. Look to him, ends of the earth, and be saved. Resist him and perish. Surprisingly, the reign and war march of the incarnate Word, our Lord Jesus, is our quietness and peace. We can be still when all is swirling because we know him who holds the storm clouds in his hand. This is his war, and he will win it by the sword of his mouth, the preaching of his everlasting gospel.

I AM

If only poverty could be abolished, every child receive a quality education, war ended, universal healthcare provided, and quality retirement guaranteed for everyone, then man's intrinsic goodness would create a society of justice and prosperity. Even the Church has manifested these utopian tendencies: monasticism, denominationalism, spiritualism, and ecumenicism. Smaller groups of believers continue to pursue the illusive dream of the perfect society through agrarianism, the perfect denomination, or reproduction of a past idealized era. Utopianism is tempting because "normal life" is far from perfect, and fallen man is an environmentalist at heart – a better environment (ecological, moral, educational, political, economic) will make men better people.

Jesus was no utopian. He called for no agrarian retreat from the cities. He did not believe in the perfectibility of human nature, even of redeemed nature this side of heaven. He did not demand the abolishment of war, encourage statist social experiments, or advocate slave revolts and union strikes. He did not call men to abandon their normal pursuits in favor of an imminent religious revolution. Men normally think of these and similar movements as precursors of great social advances, but he did not. He was rather humdrum by revolutionary standards.

At a deeper level, he was the most revolutionary figure in history exactly because he did not accept that man's environment is the source of his problems. He pointed to man as the source of man's problems. He radically rejected the notion that the source of the problem could also be the source of the solution. Man cannot save man; he cannot even help man. Jesus Christ sweeps away all our idealism (right and left), existentialism, social projects, statist hopes, "isms," and movements with the most startling direct declarations.

Seven of them are found in the gospel of John. They remain thought provoking and life-changing. They are confrontational. Each one points man to him as the source of life and salvation, of transformed lives, of joy and peace even within the boundaries of an environment that is far from utopian. They retain every ounce of their initial power and compulsion because they reject the idea that a change of scenery, society, or circumstance is necessary to have peace and justice, love and prosperity. Yet they do change man's environment because they change the ultimate problem of man's environment – man.

To the thousands that followed him to Capernaum the day after he fed them with a few scraps of bread and fish, he said, "I am the bread of life" (John 6:35,48). He is the heavenly bread, the true and safe food for the soul. Communion with him replaces man's emptiness with inexhaustible resources of grace, strength, purpose, and joy. Eat him and live; reject him and starve. Eat him and never die.

To the tens of thousands of worshippers in Jerusalem for the Feast of Booths, he stood up in the Temple, likely in the midst of the lamp-lighting ritual that symbolized the pillar of fire that led Israel through the wilderness, and proclaimed with a loud voice, "I am the light of the world" (John 9:5). He alone possesses wisdom, illumines the blind, scatters the debilitating darkness of sin, and directs those who look to him in the paths of righteousness.

To the Pharisees, the embodiment of religious pomposity and tyranny, he proclaimed, "I am the door" (John 10:7). To know the truth, one must enter through Jesus and his saving work. To know the Father, one must come through the Son. By coming to the Son, one has true knowledge, is freed from the sense of estrangement created by sin and guilt, and may come to possess firm assurance of peace with God and joy in him.

To the Pharisees again, he said, "I am the good Shepherd" (John 10:14). He does not bind heavy burdens upon the backs of struggling sinners; his yoke is easy, his burden is light. He does not run away when the wolves approach. He lays down his life for the sheep, stands before the gate to forbid pillagers from scattering his flock, knows each sheep by name, and sustains the closest possible relationship of protection and provision for those who turn from their wandering ways and humbly follow him.

To grieving Martha, incarnate life states with an authority that caused the grave of Lazarus to give up its captive, "I am the resurrection and the life" (John 11:25). Jesus does not simply point out the way to life. He does not call men to a fairy land where they think they have life by religious sentimentality and separatist forgetfulness of life's problems. He is life. In the midst of death, he is resurrection. To know him is to shed the skeletal rags of hopelessness before the grave, to find the dark cave of doom filled with brilliant light. To believe in him is to have life – present, growing, eternal, constant, perpetual life, with the bravery, confidence, and joy that comes from knowing that the keys of every graveyard are dangling from the belt of our victorious Savior.

To the disciples cowering in the upper room, he proclaims with a confidence unknown in the whispering halls of skepticism, "I am the way, the truth, and the life" (John 14:6). Jesus is the way of life for those picking their way along the miserable path of human reason. He is the truth of God for those clouded by doubts and uncertainty. He is the life of reconciliation with God through his sinless life and perfect sacrifice.

To the disciples later that same night, wondering at his commands to love selflessly, brave unknown dangers, and face his death with confidence, he says with beauty and power not attained by the entire corpus of human poetry, "I am the true vine" (John 15:1). Jesus gives the strength to persevere of which man is wholly devoid in himself. He supplies fruitfulness in place of our barrenness. This seventh "I am" is a fitting climax to the earthly teaching of our Lord. Everything man needs is found in union with him.

Those who know, believe, and love the great "I am" may have difficulty feeling the angst of modern men, why they are immersed in juvenile materialism, prey to every demagogue, religious huckster, and fad that offers meaning in a world of collapsing skepticism. Western nations are reaping what they have sown. Biological Darwinism has produced social Darwinism; it is a depressing, expensive, bloody, and futile dead end street. Enlightenment thinking has untethered human reason from its revelational moorings resulting in a void of cosmic proportions. Science without God leaves man in a cold, unmeaning world of

15

chance. He tries to fill the emptiness of unbelief with whatever promises to give light in the darkness, meaning in the insane asylum, order in the chaos. He feels guilt without hope of relief, estrangement without knowing exactly why, sexual freedom that only produces more emptiness. God is bringing the West back to square one. Yet we are not as low as we can go. Statism is stepping in to fill the void. Attempts are being made to silence dissent, to force everyone to huddle together in common frustration, anger, and self-imposed ignorance.

But Jesus remains the great "I am." His words hit us with tidal wave force. They have changed the world in the last two millennia. Sometimes those who profess to know him lose sight of them. They hold on to their systematic theologies and confessions without remembering the source of their power. They lampoon unbelief without understanding its frustration and opportunity. They are critical of obedience because they do not view the law in connection with the life of the Savior.

I AM must grip us again. He must shape our priorities, our words, our prayers, and our attitudes. He is the only person who brings us back to God, to life and light, to understanding and hope, to compassion and power. Whatever our environment may be, Jesus transforms us by his own glory that we may have abundant life, peace, and hope.

Fulcrum

Many Scriptures instruct us to think of heaven, to live in terms of heaven, to make heaven our earthly pursuit as much as our eternal goal. A few choice morsels come to mind. "Our citizenship is in heaven." "Set your affections on things above." "To depart and be with Christ is better by far." The little Scripture says of heaven intensifies rather than satisfies our desire to understand heaven and to be with our Savior there.

But what shall we do with earth until heaven? Since our citizenship is in heaven, for example, how should this guide our engagement with political movements and the philosophies of our particular age? If our mind is to be set upon the things above, does any room remain for entertainments, frivolities, or the earthly delights our flesh seems only too willing to indulge? How can we find time to pursue heaven when our life seems so filled with earth that little time remains for anything but sleep? Surely there is a balance to be found somewhere, but if so, which domain or age is the fulcrum? Heaven or earth?

This collage of competing thoughts is confused even more by the popular idea that the only relevant Christian faith is a this-world oriented faith. Various forms of Christian "isms" line up: social gospel-ism, revivalism, Reconstructionism, conservatism, and emergent church-ism are only a few of the imbalances that have weakened the Church. Each capture a greater or lesser kernel of the truth or highlight some area where our faith and life need biblical renewal, but they then elevate that little kernel to the "first things" of apostolic preaching (1 Cor. 15:3). Each is an attempt to bring heaven to bear upon earth. The implicit danger in each is earth swallowing up heaven.

Many of our imbalances and broken fulcrums share a commitment to the intrinsic goodness and moral necessity of impacting this life, its peoples, ideas, and institutions, with heaven, the gospel, and the kingdom of Jesus Christ. In the process, however, we can easily forget, and in fact have forgotten, that nothing on earth can ever compare to the glories that await in heaven (Rom. 8:18). The forms and fashions of this world are

17

passing away (1 Cor. 7:31). Fallenness cannot be expunged from history until Jesus returns to consummate and renovate (Phil. 3:20-21). At the least, these simultaneously sobering and glorious realities should shape our earthly expectations. Even the best earthly program of reform will eventually fade. Earth will not look like heaven until it is made new by the power of Jesus Christ.

In seeking to balance the glories of heaven with the claims of earth, it is an irreplaceable axiom of the Christian faith that only in the unique person of Jesus Christ are heaven and earth brought together – meaningfully, without danger to either, and in submission to the God who rules both. Our Mediator, therefore, is of necessity the eternal Son of God and the incarnate son of the virgin. He does not hold these twin natures in tension; he is a unified person with each nature retaining its essential attributes and functions. As God, he is the Creator of the world, the Word of God, and the uniquely begotten of the Father. He knows all things, forgives sins, and calms the seas by the word of his power. As man, he was born in the likeness of sinful flesh, lived a life of poverty and suffering, and died the painful, shameful, and cursed death on the cross, and rose from the dead.

He did these things as our one Mediator, the God-man. Although he was in the very form of God, he emptied himself – not of his divine nature but of his claims and glory as God – voluntarily humbled himself for our poor sake and offered himself as the propitiation for our sins. And now, having suffered and died, he has entered his glory (Luke 24:26). As the Son of man, a phrase that comes from Daniel 7:13 and emphasizes his mediatorial glory and dominion, he rules heaven and earth. He is the King of the nations and the Head of the Church. We can enter heaven only through his sacrifice and intercession. We can lead God-glorifying lives on earth only through his Spirit, word, and sacraments. In our Lord Jesus Christ, then, heaven is gained for us, and earth is restored to us. We are the heirs of all things through him. The person of Jesus Christ, therefore, is the key to heaven and earth – maintaining a holy balance between this life and the next, pursuing heaven without ascetic indifference to earth, and living on earth without forgetfulness of heaven.

The person of our Mediator teaches us that humanity can never be divinized. Men do not turn into gods. The earthly order will never turn into heaven. No human leader or world order can legitimately assume divine prerogatives. Hence, as good as any political, ecclesiastical, or familial order might be, it will still be an earthly order, with ample sins and shortcomings, inconsistencies, and weaknesses. It will disappoint and frustrate us. To the degree that it seeks submission to the Lord Jesus Christ, it can be a good order, but Jesus Christ alone is both God and man. Perhaps we should think of this as we are wringing our hands over present political realities. We should also think of this when we face our own imperfections, and those of others. We are still of the first man, of the earth, subject to all his frailty, mortality, and fallibility. While perfection is promised, it is an unattainable goal in this life.

We must for the present look to Christ Jesus for our perfection before the Father, draw from him strength unto holiness, and long for the life to come in which righteousness alone will reign. The fallenness of this life and the remaining brokenness of our individual lives do not excuse our sins and must not quench our zeal and aspirations. They must teach us to look to the God-man, Jesus Christ, for ultimate perfection, order, and peace. No government, parent, spouse, or preacher can give these things to us. They are ours in Christ in principle; they will be ours in fullness only in the new heavens and earth. Until then we longingly wait for our heavenly dwelling, for the second man, Jesus Christ, to return from heaven to perfect earth, for the abyss of God's mercy to swallow fully and finally the abyss of human sin in all its forms. As we wait on earth, we keep looking unto Jesus in heaven, the author and finisher of our faith.

Jesus Christ is now personally seated at the right hand of the Father. In practice, this life draws its significance from his reign, from heaven, and from approaching eternal realities. We cannot understand this world aright apart from his reign and kingdom. All things are to be brought in subjection to him: political philosophy, personal behavior, educational choices, finances, and marriage. All things. With limited time and resources, we must put first things first, and these first things are the beliefs, practices, and

19

Fulcrum

relationships that draw us closer to Jesus Christ, increase our knowledge and love for him, and enable us to serve him more effectively in this life.

We may find ourselves in an obscure little corner of his kingdom, without much influence or many friends. Yet, with what he has given us, we must make Jesus Christ, his kingdom and glory, the dominating pursuit of life. The only things that have any lasting significance are those things that can be brought into meaningful service to him. Everything else is negotiable and should not be given primacy in our thinking and living. We may do or not do them, depending upon circumstances and responsibilities, but they should never dominate us. What makes us indifferent to our Savior, forgetful of his claims and love, can and should be given up at a moment's notice.

Everything for which the heart legitimately longs is wrapped up in Jesus our Lord. Heaven gives meaning to our life on earth, but our life on earth will never be heaven. And if we would live better and more purposefully on earth, our only recourse is to look to Jesus, to set our minds upon his glory, and to ask him to bring the power of his reign into our lives. He does not do this in a day; we must learn patience. He will not do this without struggle; we must bear the cross. He will not do this if we allow this life to swallow the life to come, earth to diminish the glories of heaven. Our Lord Jesus Christ will have all our desire, our affection, and our dependence. He will have us endure by seeing him who is invisible. He is our wisdom, balance, our fulcrum.

In the Grip of His Glory

Sometimes faith seems unreal, disconnected from the realities of life and the offerings of secularism. This is an underlying reason for the emotional appeal of movies like The Passion and the resurgence of visual worship in the Church. They make faith seem more real, more relevant, more "here and now." The challenge of an unreal faith is perhaps a cause for the return of some Protestants to the Roman Catholic Church. Incense, works, saints, and confessionals are attractive to weak faith. It takes little faith to believe in cathedrals, papal decrees, and the Mass.

Yet even among the most mature believers, the crisis of an unreal faith often exists. Daily life is consuming. Bills must be paid. Young children require constant nurture and instruction – with patience. Sin is ever present. We know that these things are part of God's will for our lives and that perseverance through them contributes in some way to the kingdom of Christ, but there is still that longing, a hollow feeling, the desire for faith to be realized.

The essence of faith is to believe in the unseen, to hope for what we do not fully possess, to be found in Christ, and to know him (Phil. 3:9-10). Real faith cannot avoid these longings. At the same time, earthly life is a testing of this faith, and without trials faith truly is unreal. To seek something more tangible on this earth can be an attempt to evade the discipline of the cross and the reality that God is not pleased in this life to give us the full fruition of our faith. Something better awaits. The final trumpet has not sounded. It does not yet appear what we shall be.

And thus arises the temptation to give up or to develop artificial ways to make faith more real. The temptation may arise from apparent delay in the fulfillment of God's promises, external persecution, daily hardships, or personal frustration with the ongoing battle against sin. Spiritual weariness sets in, perhaps even what might be called spiritual depression. We seem to be losing our grip.

Much of the letter to the Hebrews addresses this very issue. The letter was written to believers who had experienced an earlier persecution in which they had endured joyfully the spoiling of their goods, knowing that they had in heaven a more enduring inheritance. Another persecution was on the horizon. Some were being tempted to seek an easier way. Perhaps they were asking "Has God forgotten us? How could he allow this to happen again? Are you sure that we believe the right things, that God is real, that Jesus Christ is really the Lord and Savior as we were taught? Can't we compromise a little to avoid hardship and potential ruin for our families?" These sorts of questions are implied throughout the letter. The answer is invigorating.

First, Paul focuses throughout on the greater glory of Jesus Christ. He contrasts the old and new covenants, for his audience was Jewish believers. They were perhaps inclined to revert to Judaism to avoid the reproach of Christ. He presents the glory of Christ as the eternal Son of God and the greater High Priest who offered a superior sacrifice. Unlike the old covenant sacrifices that could never take away sin, his one sacrifice has obtained our redemption (Heb. 9:12). And he is now enthroned at the right hand of the Father, as the great King-Priest who intercedes for us, rules over all things for our sake, and guarantees our full acceptance into the heavenly Holy of Holies. His glory is also greater because he was made like us in every way except for sin, endured every temptation, and is able to sympathize with us in our weakness and trials. His sympathy is not simply that of a fellow-sufferer but of the One who conquered sin, Satan, and death. He now comes to our aid with powerful compassion to enable us to overcome the world, the flesh, and the devil.

Second, the author summarizes the entire history of the old covenant world, especially its leading characters in the famous "hall of faith" in chapter 11. His main point is that every old covenant hero was sorely tested – waiting, obstacles, hardships, enemies, weariness, ostracism. Each man and woman of faith persevered by looking ahead to Jesus Christ. They all died in faith, not having received the promise but being persuaded of its reality and confessing that they were strangers and pilgrims on the earth. The end of chapter 11 is especially compelling, for in one verse he connects them to us, old to new covenant faith, people, and history

(v. 40). The promise for which they longed is now come in the person and work of Jesus Christ. His is the story; he is the living bond of vital unity between believers of every age.

Then, the author comes to that most famous verse in chapter 12: "looking unto Jesus" (v. 2). We possess so many witnesses whose lives testify to one central point. Their faith in the promise of God was the most real thing in their lives even though it can be said that they lived in hope without having received the promise: Jesus Christ. Their faith is realized in him, and the faith of the old covenant church finds its realization in the faith and faithfulness of the new covenant church. This is the climax of the letter and the grand motivation by which those facing new persecutions are to persevere. We have the reality for which the old covenant saints longed. Jesus has come – in glory as the Son of God, with power as the enthroned Mediator, with saving love and grace as the great sacrifice for our sins. If the old covenant saints could persevere in anticipation of that promise, how much more are we to be faithful since we possess its realization?

We must, therefore, run the race of faith by looking unto Jesus. Looking, seeing, and considering are important participles in the letter to the Hebrews. They are faith words. They indicate that the daily course of our lives must be one of active believing and continuous fellowship with Jesus Christ. It is true that there is more to come. Even now it does not yet appear what we shall be, but we do see Jesus (Heb. 2:9). He has become as our Mediator what we will one day become as his disciples: glorified, perfected, empowered, raised from the dead, enjoying perfect fellowship with his God and Father, reigning over all things.

We enjoy these marvelous blessings for which the old covenant saints could only long: more immediate fellowship with God on the basis of full atonement, greater confidence in prayer as God's adopted sons and daughters, more abundant testimonies to God's faithfulness, clearer knowledge that sin, Satan, and death have been conquered, the deeper joy of beholding our Savior by faith enthroned as our great King-Priest at the right hand of God. They must occupy our thoughts and our affections. We must be held in the grip of Jesus' glory. His glory must motivate our activities. It must direct our lives. But this we can do only if we are continually looking unto Jesus. Everything God has promised us has been fulfilled in him. In fellowship with him, dependence upon him, prayerful worship of him, joyful obedience to him, we possess these blessings now. We shall one day enjoy them in perfection.

Faith will seem unreal unless we are living in communion with the very real Jesus, the crucified, resurrected, and enthroned Savior. He is the reality. Faith languishes without clear, believing, adoring, loving sight of Jesus' glory. He is what makes faith real, satisfying, and transforming. Nothing can replace holding fast to him as a living person. We must put away the worldly crutches and personal idols and look to Jesus.

Odd that Paul wrote Scripture to those Hebrews. When the world is threatening to crush us, God's word is what we need. The word is Jesus' word and living voice and presence with us. The word reveals his glory. Abiding in his word is the way he abides with us and holds tightly to us (John 15:1-8). The more we yield ourselves to his word in faith and obedience, the more he reveals himself to us and dwells with us – and satisfies us (John 14:21-23; Col. 3:16). The less we are reading, praying, hearing, and obeying his word, the more we lose our grip. The more we avail ourselves of our Savior's living voice, the stronger we shall feel his grip to be upon us.

The Real Jesus

Perusing the religion section at the local bookstore will reveal a "restoration and recovery project" in full swing. Various authors of different persuasions and ability are engaged in an effort to "restore and recover" Jesus, to bring him up to date, to deliver him from past prejudice and party pride. Some leaders of this project undoubtedly feel that the liberal Jesus is too malleable, hopelessly speculative, a project of theological imagination. Yet equally unacceptable is the extreme Jesus of traditional Protestantism; he is too narrow, a product of supposedly disproved views of biblical inerrancy and infallibility. This Jesus is definitely not sufficiently broad-minded, multicultural, or Buddha-embracing. Though this project has been in process for well-over a century and is unbelief's autobiography, religionists and scholars must keep busy, justifying their tenures and influencing their colleagues. They restore and recover, hoping to find a Jesus sufficiently real to warrant their jobs but sufficiently controllable to undercut the religious extremists. It is a hopeless project.

Ironically, the real Jesus is in neither camp. He is certainly not the "demythologized, merely human, humanitarian guru of the liberal or modernistic era. This Jesus is a fiction, still popular in the older denominations, which are engaged in a life-or-death mission to maintain cultural relevance, generate revenue to repair aging houses of worship, and halt the migration of its membership. Those fleeing from these mausoleums understand that if this version of Jesus is the real one, he does not matter.

The evangelical church's Jesus suffers from too much domestication. He would not affirm much of its theology and would purge many of its temples with a whip. While better than the liberal Jesus, the evangelical Jesus often bears little resemblance to the Jesus of the Bible, for his hands are tied until he can rebuild the earthly Jerusalem, cannot save sinners unless they allow him to do so, and apparently gives his followers special permission to disobey the Bible whenever "the Spirit moves." Do not worry too much about doctrine or obedience; sit down and enjoy a latte with Jesus. You will feel better soon.

We desperately need the real Jesus. We need him because modern life is plagued by moral relativism, rising statism, and economic hardship. We need him because we are facing the twin enemies of secularism and Islam: the former condemns nothing except what condemns it, and the latter kills everything that will not embrace it. We need him because worship is in many places a circus, sermons are little more than baptized humanism, and personal morality and piety are precariously rare. We need him because he is the King and Lord of all, whose wrath is certainly kindled when his authority is not recognized and his gospel perverted either into self-affirming spirituality or grace-denying lawlessness. We need him because he is our life.

We need him because without him, we are doomed. It is inevitable. No nation, institution, or denomination has endured that has denied to him his rightful place as Lord and King of all. We need him because he is the way, truth, and life, the light of the world, the bread of life, the resurrection, the only Mediator between God and man. We need him because without him life would be exactly what the existentialists, multiculturalists, and pragmatists affirm – man alone in the universe, without morality, without a safe foundation for science, without objective meaning, personal purpose, or peace with God. The real Jesus does not need us, but we must have him or perish in the attempt to live without him.

The real Jesus is not difficult to find. Yet he is not to be found in the speculative hubris of theologians, the self-help spiritual manuals of mega-church CEO's, or the spiritual feelings of the individual. He is revealed in the Scriptures of the Old and New Testaments. Jesus affirmed the Old Testament as the very word of God with respect to which he came to change nothing (Matt. 5:17-19; 26:54; John 8:35). The New Testament he commissioned by promising to his apostles a unique indwelling and inspiration of the Holy Spirit, who would guide them into all the truth (John 16:13). The real Jesus is extremely unpopular in scholarly circles and liberal pulpits – they know he would throw them out. He is only slightly more popular among the broad evangelicals – he calls them to repent of their spiritualism and Americanism and to bow before his living, written Word.

To turn away from the Bible guarantees that the real Jesus will never be found. Never. To find, have, and keep the real Jesus, we must repent of our approach to Scripture, especially our spiritualistic pursuit of principles to make life easier or more manageable, our critical dissection of it, and our arrogant handling of it. We must also repent of our disobedience to his word for any reason – intellectual pride, clerical professionalism, skeptical disdain, spiritualistic self-sufficiency, or supposed new insights from the Holy Spirit. The rise and fall of nations, of the Church, and of the world is immediately and inseparably connected to the Bible. Reject it and commit personal and cultural suicide – or better, contract a slow, painful, and parasitic cancer. No Bible, no real Jesus. No real Jesus, pain and misery.

Oh, how the heart of the sinner clings to the real Jesus once it knows him as he reveals himself in the gospel! He is the Son of God incarnate, who condescended to take upon himself our nature in order to suffer and to redeem. He is salvation from the sin and guilt that lie behind all the frustration that fallen man feels in the depths of his being. He is the King to which all earthly kings must bow in faith and submission, the King who spells the doom of tyrants and despots, whether they cloak their actions under claims of national security or practice a less discreet policy of statism. He is the Lord of all, who upholds all things by the word of his power, directs all things by his authority, and will subdue all things beneath his feet. He is the blessed Mediator who does for us what we cannot do for ourselves, what no cadre of saints can do for us, what no spiritual leader can perform in our place – reconciliation with God, peace with God through his blood and righteousness, intercession before God as our great high Priest. He is full satisfaction for our sin, righteousness in place of our wickedness, wine for our poison, bread for our dust, water for our thirst, light for our darkness, wisdom for our foolishness, strength for our weakness. He is the Dayspring from on high that has visited us, the restorer of all things, the Lord of the new age of life and salvation which he inaugurated by destroying sin, Satan, and death by his righteousness, truth, and resurrection. This is the real Jesus.

And he can still be had. He is the same yesterday, today, and forever. He has not left us; we have left him. His power, grace, wisdom, his joy and peace, are not diminished. We do not know a portion of the power that he will exercise in our behalf to deliver us from sin, sanctify us, deliver us from tyrants, and build his international kingdom in unity through common submission to his word. We prefer to be left alone, to enjoy the septic spirituality we create by turning from his word and taming him for public consumption.

Tame him? He is the tamer. The beloved disciple bowed before him in utter humiliation. The cowardly Peter became Peter the bold once he saw his glory. Doubting Thomas confessed. Murderous Saul preached. History is a marvelous testimony to his transforming power when men and nations find him. They defy Caesar, humbly not arrogantly. Little girls prefer to be eaten by lions rather than lose him. They stick out their necks at Augsburg rather than deny him. They brave unknown shores in order to serve him. His disciples actually enjoy prayer, not as a spiritual chore but as a living communion with their life. They read his word not to find fault but to possess the manna of life. The Church can have this again, and she will.

The supposed restorers of Jesus, who are really engaged in the age-old attempt to destroy the Jesus of the Bible, do not take one important truth into consideration. They are wrong – wrong about the Bible, about the nature of truth, about the nature of Jesus. He is building his Church. He is using their perverse efforts to bring his faithful people across the world into a firmer conviction of the certainty of the words of truth, deepen their resolve to be his humble disciples, and increase their love and commitment to the real Jesus. They cannot stop him. They are myth-creators, and his reality crushes their myths. Those who believe in him, love him, and obey him will go from strength to strength, across generations, building upon and pushing out the ancient foundations until the whole earth is filled with the knowledge of his glory and the desert blossoms as the rose.

My best advice to you in these times is to cling to the real Jesus. Accept no substitutes. It will not be easy. It is the path of self-denial, cross-bearing, hard fought sanctification, patience during suffering, and living by faith. It will be challenging, for the real Jesus changes and sanctifies us, baptizes with fire to purify our hearts, and conforms us to his image. Cling to the real Jesus by being a devout student of his word, learning it and treasuring it in your heart, meditating upon it, praying it. Cling to the real Jesus through prayer. If you do not feel like praying, pray anyway, asking forgiveness for not wanting to pray and praying for a living faith that cannot but pray.

And have the real Jesus constantly before the eye of faith. Think of him in his glory at the right hand of the Father. Think of him in his humiliation on the cross. Think of him in his wisdom along the road to Emmaus. Think of him as the sustainer of the martyrs, the King of the nations, the Lord of glory. Think of his kingdom, his promises, and his strength. Think of his prayer that you will be with him and behold his glory. Think of him prayerfully, passionately, and persistently. He is your life. He is the grand reality.

Jesus Saves

"How does Jesus save us?" All believers will confess that Jesus has saved us, and that by believing in him we have forgiveness of sins and everlasting life. Some, however, cannot explain the how. Knowing how Jesus saves is a critical aspect of our faith. If we are confused or uncertain about this question, we do not really understand the gospel. Assurance of salvation will elude us, and we will not have a firm foundation to devote ourselves to God's praise and service.

The Bible is clear that we have all sinned. Its pervasive testimony to this fact is more than a statement that everyone makes mistakes. Sin, according to John, is lawlessness (1 John 5:3). Lawlessness is rebellion against God's authority. He created us to know and walk with him in joyful obedience. We turned from him and embraced Satan's lie. We lost our original righteousness and became corrupt in every part. Hence, to say that man is a sinner is to say that he is a rebel, an enemy of God (Colossians 1:21). Because man is an enemy of God by fallen nature and personal choice, he is under God's wrath. The soul that sins shall die. Death is the judicial consequence of sin, the penalty of our rebellion.

Man has tried to escape his plight from the beginning. Adam hid from God. The nations of antiquity pursued salvation through military conquest, statism, emperor worship, philosophy, the stars, and mysticism. Each of the world religions is nothing but an attempt to systematize and make respectable their rebellion through religious trappings. Roman Catholicism suggests we can be saved through membership in its communion, participation in its sacraments, and obedience to its penitential system of meritorious works.

Modern Americans are less sophisticated; we try to avoid our plight by simply denying that salvation exists beyond the will and choices of the individual. Salvation is to live authentically, in the existential now, without being subject to the judgments of others. Then, we try to drown out the screams of a guilty conscience through recreation, work, and sex. But man is who God says he is, not who man says he is. He is a sinner, a rebel, under God's wrath

- even if he is a nice person, well-educated, and politically conservative.

And so God in his mercy determined to send his only Son to atone for sin. To Adam he gave the promise of life and salvation through a coming Deliverer (Genesis 3:15). As history progressed, God gave more understanding of the Messiah's person and work. He would be a prophet to reveal God's word to us with power (Deuteronomy 18:15), a priest to provide atonement for our sins (Psalm 110:4), and a king to rule over his and our enemies (2 Samuel 7:12-13). Through him, sin would be conquered, and man saved – not through his works, his penitence, his sacrifices, or his government, but by believing in God's promised Messiah. "Messiah" means God's anointed, God's Christ, the Servant-Redeemer he would send to save sinners.

And he came. He came clothed in our flesh, for only one who shared our nature could sympathize with our infirmities, feel the weight of our plight, give to God the perfect obedience we did not, suffer the penalty that we deserved, and die as our substitute. He also came as fully God. Only as God could he make intercession for us in the presence of God behind the curtain of the heavenly Holy of Holies. Only as God could he endure the full weight of divine justice and satisfy its demands. Only as God would his obedience, sufferings, and death have an intrinsic worth and saving efficacy that would be sufficient to atone for sin and make God's people righteous. Accordingly, there is no salvation without a human Savior. There is also no salvation without a divine Savior. And Jesus of Nazareth, the Christ of God, is both of these, two natures in one person.

And he died. The Bible presents his death as the substitution that God provided. He did not die as a result of his own sins but to atone for ours. He died as a sacrifice, to satisfy divine justice and to obtain our forgiveness. God is merciful, but he is never merciful at the expense of his justice. Since we could not satisfy God's judgment, Jesus became our propitiation (1 John 2:2). He satisfied God's justice by means of his blood. He died the painful and shameful death of the cross, sinking so low because our sins had sunk us into filth and judgment. Jesus Christ saved us at the cross, not so much because of the horror of his particular death but because his appointed death in place of sinners was his taking the full weight of our judgment upon his own holy back.

And he rose. The cross alone cannot save us. By raising his beloved Son from the dead, God declares to all that he fully accepts the sacrifice of his Son in the place of sinners, that his justice has been satisfied, and that all who trust in his Son will not only be forgiven but declared righteous by his obedience (Romans 4:25). By raising his Son from the dead, God declares him to be the appointed Deliver. He proclaims to us in the gospel that by believing upon him, we are justified, declared righteous before God on the basis of his obedience imputed to us and his shed blood cleansing us.

And he ascended. We tend to overlook this aspect of how Jesus saves us. His ascension was his monarchical procession to the right hand of God (Acts 2:30-36). There he is not only the King of men and nations who will subdue all his enemies beneath his feet by his word and Spirit, but he is also our sympathetic high priest through whom we have confidence to draw near to God and daily assurance that all our sins will be forgiven when we come unto God through faith in his Son. Jesus saves us as much by his advocacy and "appearing in the presence of God for us" as he did by his death and resurrection.

This is how Jesus saved us and is saving us. It is an old message, but it is the message the world still needs. Our sexual freedom has not brought salvation – only disease, the end of consecrated marriage, flagrant immorality, and perversion. Powerful governments have not saved us; wars, corruption, and death follow in their wake. Science has not saved us – it has brought ethical confusion, universal skepticism concerning ultimate truth, and the chilling specter of technological sophistication without any moral compass. Entertainment has not saved us. What kind of life is it to live out fantasy through the lives of shallow celebrities and jaundiced athletes masquerading as cultural icons of success?

Only Jesus can save us. And knowing how he has saved us is critical to our daily assurance that he has indeed saved us. It also leads us to him as the living Savior from whom we receive grace and strength to live whole and purposeful lives in gratitude to God and loving service to men.

The Joy of Jesus

Though he was the Man of sorrows, we should never think that sorrow dominated our Lord's emotional life. It is true that his appointed office was to drink the cup of God's judgment against sin. He bore our griefs, carried our sorrows, and took our weaknesses upon himself. Every healing, raising, and feeding cost him an ocean of tears at sin's devastation and his soul's compassion. He never offered to his Father what cost him nothing. Between the wine at Cana and the blood at Calvary, he spared no tears or groans for the plight of sinners. He endured every pain, temptation, and trial that was necessary for him to sympathize with us and to be the sinless, worthy Lamb of God. Go with him to Gethsemane and Golgotha, and you will see how low our sin brought him. In both places, he felt the sorrows of hell and the pains of death with a magnitude that almost killed him in the Garden and did kill him at Calvary. There was no other way for sinners to be redeemed except by his being crushed in their place.

Even so, it was not sorrow that dominated him. Our salvation cost our Redeemer's blood and tears, but it flowed from our Redeemer's joy. It is against the backdrop of his sorrows that the sun of his joy blindingly shines. It was joy that empowered him to endure the cross (Heb. 12:2). In the fullest sense, the joy of the Lord was his strength. How could he whose lot was suffering and humiliation have such joy? This is an important question, for he speaks on that last night of his joy being fulfilled in us (John 15:11). What kind of joy did he have? From whence did it come? How may we have it?

The first truth we must recognize about our Lord is that he trusted God implicitly, with every ounce of his being. God was his life. The mockery heaped upon him at the cross – "He trusted God" (Matt. 27:43) – was far truer than anyone standing there could possibly fathom. God was his Father in a constant, deeply personal, omnipresent sense. He lived before the face of God. He saw his Father's hand and will behind every sorrow, temptation, and commonplace experience. "If you are the Son of God," Satan taunted him, "Command these stones to become bread." No, he responded, I will trust my Father's word (Matt. 4:4). Did the seas rage? "Why are ye so fearful, O ye of little faith" (Matt. 8:26)? Do you not remember that God sits as King above the floods? Peter tempted him to turn from the path of the cross, but he said, "Get behind me, Satan; you do not savor the things that be of God" (Matt. 16:23). At the last, when the disciples drew their swords to defend him, he said, "The cup which my Father hath given me, shall I not drink it" (John 18:11). He trusted his Father at every dreadful step that led him to the cross.

During that last week in Bethany, he spoke of his soul being troubled because his hour was come (John 12:27). With his next breath, he said, "But for this reason I come to this hour. Father, glorify thy name." We find him praying the same in John 17. Jesus's joy is based upon his absolute, immovable trust that his life was directed by God in every detail, every relationship, and every hardship. If Jesus' joy is to be fulfilled in us, as he said, we must gain much larger views of God. We can gain them, for Jesus has opened heaven to us. He has brought us near to God. We can grow in confidence that God is always with us, directing all things for our good and his glory, and that everything is an occasion for him to reveal his faithfulness, power, and love to us. As we gain greater trust in God, we shall have more of Jesus' joy.

The second truth about Jesus's joy is his obedience to the Father's will. He clearly connected obedience, love, and joy in John 15:9-11. In Psalm 40:6-8, which is directly applied to our Lord in Hebrews 10:7-8, he said, "I delight to do your will, O my God." As our Mediator, he entered into our condition. He walked as we must walk: in obedience to God. He learned obedience through suffering and submission (Heb. 5:8-9), and therefore his joy was mounting with each obedient step to his ultimate act of obedience. Although the closer he drew to that hour, the heavier his burden became, men were drawn to him, especially sufferers. He did not practice John's austerity but came "eating and drinking."

It is much easier for us to think that holiness requires an ascetic removal from this life, a narrow strictness that makes us suspicious of too much joy, lest we become contaminated or

The Joy of Jesus

distracted. Jesus puts the lie to this philosophy by his challenging example. Joy is not found in isolation from the world but in entering fully into each day's opportunities for doing good, laughing, and simple delight in the common goodness of God to his creatures. We should never fear that such joys are somehow unspiritual. Look at how Jesus embraced the children, turned the water into wine, and generally went about doing good so that men wanted to seek him out. Men do not usually seek out austere individuals. In all these instances, Jesus knew that the secret of joy was the path of obedience. God can be obeyed and glorified and enjoyed in every setting that is not intrinsically sinful.

Never has there been a more challenging joy than Jesus's joy in obeying his Father! Joy in obedience? We have isolated joy from obedience and have lost both in the process. As obedience feeds joy in God, so joy empowers obedience. We often think that joy is life going as we planned or being as free as possible from the vexations of life. Joy is going somewhere, doing something fun, all set to music that makes us forget that this is not really joy but escape from responsibility and flight from maturity. Our Lord teaches us a more solid joy: obeying God. To recover this, we shall have to recover some sense of the "deeper magic" of the universe: that God created us to find our deepest satisfaction, emotional fulfillment and stability in obeying him. Run from this, however you may justify it, or think it too hard, and you run from joy. Jesus' joy may be enjoyed in a very busy life, amid squawking children, or living with an insensitive husband or a cold wife. Joy is God. "In thy presence is fullness of joy." There is not an amusement park in heaven. God is there, and God is joy. To obey him is to live in harmony with the cosmic purpose that lies behind all things. Where our lives are flat, joyless, purposeless, it is likely because we are not obeying God.

It seems impossible that joy could be so simple and straightforward. It must be complicated, for life is complicated, is it not? Sin complicates life; obedience simplifies it. Sin creates many problems and psychoses, as we see in our society. Obedience brings peace and joy to our souls as nothing else can. Trust the example of our Savior. "I always do those things that please my

Father" (John 8:29). Here is emotional stability. Do you want it in your home? Obey. Husband, love your hard to love wife; wife, obey your hard to obey husband. You do not need a conference to tell you that it will be difficult, or a library of books to justify all the reasons that in your particular case, simple obedience to God is insufficient and that there are very good reasons for straying from Jesus' path. Obey. Obey and you will sing with Paul and Silas. Obey and you will speak boldly like the early church when she was told not to speak in Jesus' name. Obey God with thankful, joyful hearts, whatever the cost, however difficult it may seem, and Jesus will fulfill his joy in you. "If ye know these things, happy are ye if ye do them" (John 13:17).

There is another source of Jesus' joy. He always hoped in his Father. Hope is the assurance that what God has promised is absolutely true. Hope in God's word is the helmet that protects the head from doubt and uncertainty (1 Thess. 5:8). Hope is the assurance that God is always faithful to his promises and that whatever is happening to us, he is working out his purposes. Hope gives resolution in duty, comfort in adversity, and peace in tribulation. Never did Jesus doubt the certainty of God's promises. He lived by every word of God. Hope sustained his joy on the cross, even when he was forsaken as our substitute. He knew that he was the covenant and that his blood spilt would seal the covenant. It is one thing to hope in life, when everything is going along as it should. Facing death, judicial death, death as judgment and hell for sin, Jesus yielded his spirit to the Father. He voluntarily resigned his life. How could he do this? How could he do it joyfully? He hoped. He was assured that the God who had been with him in life would take care of him in death, even in that death.

Grow in hope, child of God, and your joy will grow deeper, more mature, less tossed by the tides of trouble. God will take care of you. He has promised. He always fulfills the good word of his promise. Feed upon his promises. Think about them constantly. "Why art thou cast down, O my soul? And why art thou disquieted in me? Hope thou in God: for I shall yet praise him, who is the health of my countenance, and my God" (Ps. 42:5,11).

The Last Miracle

Aroused from their dazed and troubled slumbers, the disciples, now reduced by one, watched with amazement as the Lord went forth to meet his captors. "Whom seek ye," he boldly asks (John 18:7). He will not be taken on their terms, under cover of night, but forces the issue and will have them publicly identify their intended victim. They must seize him alone, for he will lose none of his. He is the great High Priest now arrived at the hour for which he came, resolved to obtain our redemption, ready to crush the serpent's head. The eleven, his tormentors, and the world must know this encounter was no accident. Yes, this is "their hour and the power of darkness" (Luke 22:53), but, as the Captain of our salvation, he will direct their evil course according to the will of his Father and the requirements of our salvation.

Upon their "Jesus of Nazareth," his "I am" – not by magic but by momentary unveiling of his divine presence and power – throws his would-be captors to the ground (John 18:8). He will have them know just who he is upon whom they dare to lay hands and that had he willed he could destroy them in an instant. Twelve legions of angels – perhaps one for each of the disciples and for himself – would at his word appear with drawn, fiery swords. But he came to save the world, not to destroy it. It must nevertheless be seen and heard that he gave himself into the hands of wicked men at his own initiative, without any other compulsion than that of submission to his Father and love for his sheep. Only hereby could he be the willing scapegoat for our sins and by his voluntary suffering and death be our acceptable substitute.

Judas, also, now fully the son of perdition, falls to the ground: last, fleeting opportunity, O doomed one, to recall the divine glory of him whom you claimed to love and serve and the heavenly words you received from his lips for three years. You, at least, sense this "I am" to be no joke but the revelation of irresistible, invincible power. No, you have pledged yourself to the devil; in smoldering, angry pride, you will not even now, as the hammer strikes the bell of your eternal damnation, forsake your evil promise. The kiss planted, the last deception uttered, "Hail,

Master," the doom sealed (Matt. 26:49). How horrible to be the author of the most horrific act ever to seep from man's fallen heart – in the face of divine glory and undying love!

The traitor's kiss signals to the disciples that something is horribly wrong. Betray? That word from our Lord's mouth removes in an instant the lingering hold of their grogginess. Odd that our Lord's urging them to join him in prayer and begging for their support could not arouse them, but this "betray" alerted them to an imminent danger, the threat of which had haunted them throughout the evening. Still senseless to the true nature of the "power of darkness" besieging our Savior, they think to draw swords. Somewhere in the recesses of memory, the Lord's recent words came to them: "And he that hath no sword, let him sell his garment and buy one" (Luke 22:36). How silly and misplaced our zeal and attempts at warfare when we do not understand the true enemy. Sin, Satan, and his evil henchmen cannot be met and overcome by the strength of steel.

Still stinging from the rebuke to his pride, Peter thinks to himself that here is his chance to make good on his promise never to forsake the Lord, to die with him if necessary. How little he understands this hour, the nature and power of darkness, the vanity of his own heart, and the demands of our salvation! Wildly swinging, he severs the ear of Malchus, one of the high priest's servants. In this momentary mayhem, our salvation hung in the balance. It would have been easy for a slaughter to have ensued: the disciples slain and lost, our Lord's mission reduced to one more in a long line of rebels and would be messiahs trying to overthrow the existing power and establish their own regime.

Witness our Lord's total control of the situation, He steps into the fray unarmed. "Let us go" (Mark 14:42). He declares a truce to this melee. "Are you come out, as against a thief, with swords and clubs to take me? I was daily with you in the temple, and you took me not: but the Scriptures must be fulfilled" (vv. 48-49). You have no armed power over me. You could have taken me many times, for my ministry has been very public. You could not take me by human force then. You will not now. I will give myself into your hand by my own will, for you could never take me otherwise. I will lose none of mine in this fashion.

And they yield to him, the captors to the captive, the henchman of Satan to the lone voice of the lowly Savior. Shall we ever fear the power of men over the righteous or think to further Christ's kingdom purposes by our desperation and wrath? Satan, that arch-deceiver, ever tries to confuse the issue, reduce salvation to political machinations and rebellion, obscure the gospel under a cloud of unwise zeal on the part of Christ's professing friends. Jesus Christ will have none of it. Never must we allow our judgment to be clouded, even in an extreme hour of what appears to us to require worldly effort and dependence upon the arm of the flesh. As with our Head, our complete security always lies in total dependence upon the will, power, and protection of God, our only wisdom in submission to his word.

To Peter he commanded, "Put up your sword into the sheath: the cup which my Father has given me, shall I not drink it" (John 18:11)? Earlier in the evening he had told the disciples to acquire swords and begin carrying money. They had no need of these things when he was with them, for his immediate presence and the inauguration of his kingdom were enjoyed and confirmed by his total provision for their needs without the ordinary means of preservation and protection. He would soon be physically removed from them, and they would need to take thought for these things.

But not yet: he is still with them. Having won the battle in the garden, he is prepared to drink the cup of God's wrath against us. Put up your swords; you are interfering with my cup, dirtying my sacrifice, confusing my gospel. Even more: "All they that take the sword shall perish with the sword," which Matthew records our Lord saying to Peter at this moment (Matt. 26:52). You cannot further my kingdom purposes with human weaponry; my earlier admonition to acquire swords pertains to personal defense, not to silly attempts to promote my gospel at sword point, by enmeshing yourself in the vacillating political movements and rebellions of the world. Put the sword away, Peter; like me, submit to the will of God. Let God further his kingdom and show his power in the way of the cross. Only my blood will save you, not the shedding of man's blood.

The last miracle: he touched Malchus' ear and healed him. The armed bands and the misguided disciples created confusion; Jesus stood as calm healer. Hate and fear fill the air. Wearied by the deadly combat in the garden and the dark cross looming before him, he healed one of his ignorant enemies. Behold his love in the midst of man's fury, his clarity in the midst of man's confusion, his gentleness in the midst of man's anger. This last miracle is perhaps the clearest of all in terms of defining the nature of his kingdom, especially occurring at this place, in this hour. His is not a kingdom of sword's loud clash but of love's tender sacrifice, not of man's fury but of heaven's peace – through the cross, through love, through doing good to one's enemies.

Moments of great crisis sometime arise in our lives and in the world, when the kingdom purposes of God seem to hang by a thread – or at least we think they do. Something must be done. We search for the weapons at hand, those that men commonly use to defend themselves, escape, or destroy others. For some, it is the cache of weapons; for other, it is pietistic retreat from the world; for still others, it is political machinery, which in many ages has been the apparent de facto power on earth. As our Savior said, there is certainly a time both to own and use swords and guns, primarily in personal defense. We need occasional retirement from the demands of service and sacrifice, as our Lord is recorded to have sought on occasion. And political involvement, where its platform is Scripture righteousness and its aim the reign of Christ, is good and necessary. But each of these has limits, and none of them is the primary weapon of our warfare.

Witness our Lord; hear his words. My kingdom is different. "If my kingdom were of this world, my servants would fight, that I should not be delivered to the Jews" (John 18:36). If his kingdom were of this world, it would advance in the customary fashion of human kingdoms and movements – with swords, guns, the might and intrigue of men. Fundamentally, the last miracle teaches us that we must love our enemies, do good to those who hate us, and pray for those who treat us with reproach and disdain. We shall not

41

out-shout them, out-gun them, and out-maneuver them in worldly affairs. Even if we could, would our Savior's kingdom purposes be truly advanced and established? Hear him: "All who take the sword shall perish by the sword." Fight the world's way and suffer the consequences. Depend upon worldly methods, and they will crush you.

Do nothing? Silly response: this is to be like Peter, who thought the way to prove allegiance to Jesus Christ was to pound one's chest, measure human against human strength, and reject the cross as God's path to salvation and victory. Did Jesus do nothing at this hour? He had spent much of the previous evening in prayer. He went forth boldly to meet his captors. He was governed by God's word. Yes, but he was different. True, he was the Son of God and Savior of sinners, but he is our Head, and "he that says he abides in him ought to walk as he walked" (1 John 2:6). He walked in the strength of prayer and submission to his Father. He walked in surrender to the cross the Father had laid upon him. He walked in love toward his enemies. This is our walk, if we are wise in him, if we would have a share in the "greater works" he performs from the right hand of the Father, for he has poured forth his Spirit and invites us to enjoy his power and presence until the end of the age.

Therefore, in the midst of whatever else we think will be effective and necessary to fight his battle in our times, are we walking in his clear steps. Are we using the weapons that demolish strongholds? Prayer is among the deadliest to God's enemies, for believing, fervent, and kingdom prayer rises as incense to God's throne and is emptied back down on earth in the form of judgment upon his enemies and deliverance to his church. Show me a man who fights but does not pray like this, votes but does not pray like this, reads his devotionals but does not pray like this, listens to sermons but does not pray like this, and I will show you a very weak man, easy prey for Satan's attacks upon him personally, in his home, and in his work.

Is the cross our only boast? This is the stumbling-block of history, the dividing line between men, the power of God unto salvation, and the path of discipleship. We are called by our Savior to bear this cross, his cross. We are never to forget our lowliness, the shame of our sin, the price the Son of God paid for our salvation. The cross must control our thoughts, color our language, and consume our relationships – even with unbelieving men. Their pride, rebellion, and darkness are not scattered by our better arguments, platforms, sense of history, and vision – but only by the Son of God plunging the stake of life into their hearts. All Christian piety worthy of the name, Christian political activity, and Christian endeavor of whatever kind uphold the cross and resurrection of Jesus Christ as man's only hope. His cross defines our expectations, our methods, and our path. It did his, and the servant is not above his Master.

And are we loving? It should strike us deeply that Jesus' last miracle was not calling down those twelve legions of angels, walking through the midst of his enemies unscathed as he did on another occasion, or making Peter's sword flash forth with fire. He healed an enemy; he healed a nobody. Satan was roaring. Our Savior's enemies brandished swords. His disciples were joining the world's frenzy. Jesus stilled the storm yet again, paused momentarily, and showed love. Should not this have utterly confounded them, at least Malchus?

Wait a minute! Insurrectionists do not treat their enemies with compassion. This is the supposedly dangerous man we have come to arrest? He poses no threat to us; he heals his enemies so they can fight again. Who is this? He is the lover of sinners, the Savior of sinners. He is unlike any other. And he calls us to walk in the fellowship of his love and compassion to miserable, sin-blinded, sin-crazed men. "By this all men know that you are my disciples, if you have love one to another" (John 13:35). Do we? Are we loving our enemies, praying for them, endeavoring to do them good, blessing those who curse us? Jesus Christ – his true gospel, the nature of his reign and kingdom, the uniqueness of his person, the glory of his church – will be lost in the shuffle of human confusion unless his last miracle so grips us that we seek from the Father a heart like our Lord's. Gain everything else, but lose love, and we lose everything. Defeat the political regime du jour and beat the heretics but lose love, and we lose our soul. We will lose the gospel. We will lose Jesus Christ.

The Last Miracle

Follow our Lord through the rest of that dark night until early the next morning when he laid down his life upon the cross. For whom? For his enemies, including us. That we are now his friends is only because love satisfied divine justice, obtained our eternal redemption, set up his kingdom of grace and glory. Love saved the world. The last miracle shows us the way to walk in the path of victory, of true usefulness in whatever particular corner of the vineyard to which the Lord has called us, whether in the halls of political power or in a cubicle of obscurity.

~2~
They Crucified the Lord of Glory

Mystery, Wonder, and Awe

We are regularly confronted with men who feel competent to tell us what is wrong with the world. If we only had more educational programs for the poor, after school care for children of single parents, a more effective UN presence in oppressed nations, then crime, poverty, and ignorance could be defeated. Conservatives tells us that government is the problem, deficit spending, high taxation, and globalism. More sensitive souls identify racism, prejudice, environmental abuse, and discrimination as the source of the evils in the world. Everyone has an opinion on the nature of the problem. Blind men can see some of the symptoms of the disease, but they cannot see or identify the disease itself. It is sin, judicial estrangement from God, and lack of saving faith in Jesus Christ as the way, truth, and life.

Even some corners of Christ's Church have lost any proper sense of mystery, wonder, and awe that comes from kneeling at the foot of his cross and understanding the significance of our Savior's death. This loss, more than any other single factor, also explains our lack of power. The cross is not only our only legitimate boast, but it is also the one weapon before which Satan must flee. Once we turn away from the glory of the cross, our preaching loses its compulsion, our worship its humble gratitude, and our lives the motivation for obedience. All is rubbish if we lose sight of Jesus Christ, and him crucified.

Part of this loss is to be explained by the manner in which the cross has been grossly misinterpreted by liberal scholars, pastors, and Christians, who are often embarrassed by blood atonement, crave the acceptance of the world, and are unwilling to glory in the sufferings of a crucified Savior. Thus, the cross has been reduced to the death of a great martyr, an unsuccessful revolutionary, or a misunderstood rabbi. The loss of mystery and awe before the foot of the cross is sometimes to be explained by the gross materialism of our age, the rise of atheistic science, which leaves no room for the Christian God, and the entrenchment of radical pluralism, which views the cross as simply one significant religious event in the history of man's attempt to understand our ultimately unknowable universe. And, we cannot fail to mention that the glory of Christ will be tarnished in the life of the Church to the degree that we allow the cares of the world and the deceitfulness of riches to choke out the word. The cross must be everything, or it will become nothing.

Pause again, believer, before the foot of the cross, and marvel at its meaning. It is the most significant event in the history of the world. To appreciate the cross, however, we must see something of our condemnation apart from the cross. It was sin that nailed Jesus to the cross – not sin in general or the gross examples of sin that all despise. It was the sins of anger, gossip, manipulation, lust, anger, meanness, miserliness, lies, worldliness, and discontent. It was our sins and core sinfulness, the depravity that defines us from conception. On the cross, Jesus bore the penalty these and every sin deserve and would have received had not God intervened to provide an acceptable substitute to satisfy his perfect justice. The reason men do not marvel before the cross is that they misunderstand sin. It is trivialized, excused, mocked, and treated as a "mistake" rather than an affront to God. If you would regain a sense of wonder before the foot of Jesus' cross, you must reconsider the ugliness, treachery, and unbelievable ingratitude associated with every sin.

Consider the cross from the perspective of God. He intervened. He did not leave fallen man under sin's dominion and judgment. Incomparable love is manifested at the cross as well as inflexible justice. They intersected in those crosspieces one dark day two thousand years ago. Again, however, men no longer understand love. Love is sex. Love is emotion. Love is a feeling. Love is acceptance. God's love, on the other hand, is the compassionate action of his mercy and goodness to sinners that deserve justice, pity toward those that deserve his wrath, and omnipotence savingly exercised toward the impotent. Love is gracious sacrifice.

As long, however, as there is a self-help section at the local bookstore, as long as love is viewed in shallow, selfish, and humanistic terms, men will never bow before the cross, broken, crying, and utterly humbled before the amazing love of God. They will never deny self, be emptied of vain efforts toward self-improvement, or freed from the delusion of love masquerading as lust, indulgence, and ego.

It does not have to be this way. The Church and the world can experience another reformation of thought and life. It will. Jesus is praying that all men will know that the Father has sent him (John 17:23). I pray we are not standing in the way of this reformation. We are unless we are bowing in wonder before the cross. We are if we have lost the consuming passion of Paul: "And God forbid that I should glory save in the cross of our Lord Jesus Christ" (Gal. 6:14). And, "For me to live is Christ" (Phil. 1:21).

This is the problem in the world today. We do not hear the thunder of Calvary, echoing the justice of God across the heavens. We do not feel the darkness that descended that day, as the Father turned his face from his Son so that he would not have to turn his face from us. We do not see the blood flowing from his pierced side, testifying that redemption is accomplished, Satan defeated, and the Judge satisfied. And having lost these sanctified convictions, we carefully place the gospel story in the back of our minds, glad we are not going to hell, but unable to create and sustain the zeal, sacrifice, and boldness that transformed a humble band of Galilean fisherman and women into heralds of the day of salvation from sin, darkness, chaos, and tyranny.

Child of God, let it never be said of you that you have lost the mystery, wonder, and awe of the cross. Return to Calvary often in your thoughts and prayers. Though they did not know it, when the Romans dropped the cross in the earth that day, God planted his glorious flag of salvation. It is that flag to which all will rally, to which all the nations will throng. This occurs as the Church recovers and retains the adoring belief that she owes everything to the blood of Jesus Christ. It occurs when our daily lives are pursued with the eye of faith fixed upon our Savior's humble and now exalted standard. It occurs as we live in the joy that every promise of God is ours because the Son of God incarnate bled and died for our salvation.

Mystery, Wonder and Awe

Lose everything else, but do not lose the wonder of the cross. Sell everything for this pearl, but do not sell your soul to the world for a few crumbs of supposed respectability and acceptance. It will not profit us if we gain the whole world but lose our own soul. The only way to keep our soul is to have and hold the mystery, wonder, and awe of Jesus Christ, and him crucified. Its shame is our glory and our salvation.

As White as Snow

The Christian faith makes the most remarkable claim ever heard. Through faith in Jesus Christ, a man, any man, the most evil man in the world, can be immediately, fully, and eternally forgiven of his sins. He need add nothing to the finished work of Jesus Christ – no good deeds, mystical encounter with God, rite, or ritual. He need only believe in his heart and confess with his mouth that he is a justly condemned sinner before the holy God, that his only hope is in the mercy of God freely offered and given through Jesus Christ, and that Jesus Christ is Lord, his only hope in life and death. Whatever his past life, connections, or crimes, he may be made as white as snow: forgiven of his sins, cleansed from their guilt and penalty, justified by Christ's imputed righteousness, and adopted by the Holy Spirit into the family of God.

This claim is remarkable, for no one else is making it. Roman Catholicism does not make it, for its entire system of justification is based upon uncertainty – even if I do everything prescribed by the church, its whole litany of penance, confession, and ritual, I will likely do a stint in purgatory before being admitted to heaven, and this only if I do not commit a mortal sin. The world religions do not make this claim – each is a pyramid, a shell game, with initiates confusedly scattered up and down the chain of being, the path of transcendental enlightenment, or the ladder of good works. Christian spin-offs or cults do not make this claim – their various redemptive systems are a jumbled combination of good works, Christ and personal merit, and allegiance to the venerated, infallible founder. Each depends upon creating, not removing, the sense of guilt and alienation from God, for followers will be the more wedded to programs, acts of penitence, and human leaders to the degree that redemption remains in doubt. This also explains the reason no Christian cult believes in the perseverance and preservation of the saints; salvation can be lost. This keeps the devotees in line. Their systems are designed to make man feel farther from God, not closer, more uncertain of final salvation, not more confident. They make slaves, not liberated, courageous, and loving men gratefully devoted to the glory of God.

As White as Snow

Christianity's claim is remarkable because everyone is seeking a perverted version of what the Christian gospel offers, and Jesus Christ gives: reconciliation with God and the restoration of man. Our political systems are based upon the idea that man has core deficiencies – politically, socially, and economically defined sins – that can be checked and corrected only by an all-wise, all-provident, and all-sufficient state. Our educational systems are similarly redemptive, as are our social programs, foreign policies, and planned economy: salvation by money, humanitarianism, militaristic intervention, and central planning. Our ecological efforts are redemptive; man feels that he can only save himself by saving his environment.

What else is globalism but the same fear that prompted the erection of the original global tower at Babel – the attempt to hide from the face of God and to escape from the uneasy sense of divine scrutiny and judgment? Man feels better able to do this if everyone is part of a global system: equally vulnerable, equally watched, and equally mediocre. Even the professed atheist, who vociferously denies any concern with God and redemption, cannot even curse without taking God's name upon his lips. By profaning the name of the denied-God, he would assume power over that God, the power to escape, deny, and eradicate God's claims upon his life. Everywhere one looks, man is haunted by his sense of alienation from God. His gnawing conscience screams for redemption.

Man's religiousness is not a new observation; it is as old as man himself. It is only the modern secularist who would deny this. Secularism, however, is the reason for our ubiquitous litigation, broken families, rudeness, and economic cannibalism, by which we spend and consume everything now without a thought for the future. The denial of God always leads to theft, isolation, self-indulgence, and dog-eat-dog chaos in every human relation. These tragedies are inescapable for man's creation in God's image is inescapable. God will be worshipped and served, or man will be lost and miserable. The breakdown of modern society is thus a strikingly clear proof not only of God's existence but also that his wrath is being revealed from heaven against every form of ungodliness, against those who worship and serve the creature rather than the Creator.

Because God is God and has revealed himself in the world and in the hearts of all men, none of our redemptive schemes to improve education, save the environment, preserve ourselves from economic decline, establish democracy in the world, and strengthen our families will succeed. They are not succeeding because we live in a world created and governed by God, whose word alone is life and whose holy purposes are accomplished on earth as they are in heaven. In him we move, live, breathe, and have our very existence. When man denies God as his ultimate environment, when he denies God as his life, misery, confusion, and self-destructive programs ensue.

And thus, our sense of alienation, our craving for redemption, is explained. We have revolted from the law of our creation, which is to love, know, and glorify God. We have lain with strange gods, which neither we nor our fathers have known. We have sown to the wind and are reaping the whirlwind. We have rejected the fountain of living waters and formed broken cisterns that cannot hold water. Rebellion against God does not mean man ceases to be concerned with redemption. The longing for reconciliation with God is desperately intensified the more we push away the light of his truth. Conscience becomes more agitated and implacable because it will not be satisfied by trifles, excuses, and forgetfulness. God has made us for himself, and our hearts are miserably restless until they rest securely in him.

And rest we can. Unlike every other world religion, cult, or secular program, Christianity's remarkable claim is that man cannot mount up to God but that God condescends to man. He reaches down to us, spiritually dead, rebellious, and undeserving though we are. He did this through his Son. Through Jesus Christ's expiatory death, sinless life, and victorious resurrection, we are washed from our sins and reconciled to God. The righteousness God legitimately demands from his creatures is bestowed freely as a gift. By faith in Jesus, we are cleansed, reconciled, redeemed, and restored. We are washed as white as snow. Nothing can or need be added to the finished work of Christ. It need only be received through faith in the promise of God that is proclaimed in the gospel of Jesus Christ.

This gospel is the harbinger of hope for man. It puts an end to tyranny and messianic states because man is no longer consumed with fear of death, of man, and of nature. He does not cast a grim look to the heavens and think God is his enemy, the foreboding presence from which he cannot escape. God is reconciled; I am clean. Let man do what he will; God is my reconciled Rock and impregnable Fortress, not the schemes and promises of the dead.

The gospel of Jesus Christ also puts an end to personal frustration and despair. I cannot do enough; I know I cannot pull myself up to heaven. I am a sinner; my fundamental problem is not without but within. So much for the world religions, who either try to mount up to heaven on the wings of mysticism or by treading the dark valley of man-made ritual and moralism. So much for pseudo-Christianity's paralyzing allegiance to systems of penance, purgatory, and blind allegiance to very fallible leaders. I will worship God not as a slave of fear and self-justification but as an adopted son of the Lord of glory. I will sing a new song to the Lord, wear his shining robe of righteousness, and come to him with confidence through Jesus Christ.

Trusting Jesus as Savior also puts an end to the destructive pursuit of perfectionism while at the same time empowering true obedience. I am not made more right with God by a godly life; I can be no more right with him than I am through Jesus Christ, his sacrifice and righteousness. I cannot be whiter than snow, cleaner than his blood has made me. Yes, I want to please my heavenly Father, obey his Word, and be a faithful disciple of Jesus Christ. Yet, this is prompted by gratitude not by guilt, by love not dread. And when I fall, which I most certainly will, I cover myself again in the snowy righteousness of Jesus Christ. One drop of his blood falls upon my blackness, one glance of the Father's love for me through his Son, and all is white again. As white as snow.

Father, Forgive Them

Push aside for a moment the weariness of our warfare, with its scars of past defeat and anxieties of present conflict. Let faith rise above the paralysis of guilt; put aside pettiness, prejudice, and party-pride. Let righteous indignation and soul vexation take a brief and much-needed respite. Then, the most astounding words ever uttered upon this earth might come to us again, a sentence so precious, a light so sublime, a love so pure. The words were spoken at the point of deepest, darkest blackness, at once the lowest and highest point of human history, gasped by a soul humbled, cursed, and tormented beyond description. These words are life from the dead. "Father, forgive them, for they know not what they do."

Understand that our Lord was not simply forgiving the Jews and Romans. This interpretation ignores and debases what took place on that blood-drenched hill. Yes, there were human instruments of cruelty and injustice at work, of spiritual blindness without equal but in hell. But our hands were nailing him there just as surely as those of the Romans at the instigation of the Jews. It was our treacheries and treasons that brought the Son of God, the Beloved of the Father, to such an end. It was our ingratitude and rebellion – in the Garden and in life – that crucified the Lord of glory. It was our deception, pride, and self-love. He put himself upon the cross because the wages of sin is death, because the soul that sins must die, because he took upon himself the sword of divine justice for his sheep, for the world.

He said, "Father." How can his filial confidence be reconciled with "My God, my God, why hast thou forsaken me" (Matt. 27:46)? Like his person, his work was multi-faceted, deeply layered. As the burnt offering for sin, he was fully conscious of the separating reality of sin. God is of purer eyes than to behold iniquity (Hab. 1:13). To bear away sin, to satisfy divine justice for sin, he had to become the sacrificial lamb and the scapegoat, at once the offeror and the offering, the priest and the victim. In one act, he had to suffer hell and endure the misery of eternal separation from the comforting, life-giving presence of God.

Unspeakable grief, agony of soul, pain of body: each he bore, more fully than we can ever know in those hours on the cross. In a true sense, he was forsaken; he had to be forsaken. Sin subjects us to being utterly forsaken by God, which is the very worst the image-bearer of God can suffer. It would be easier to live without sunlight and air than to live without God.

At the same time, and here we must bow before deep, unfathomable mystery, he remained confident of his Father's love. "For this cause I have come into the world," he said. The horrors engulfing and the sword of justice striking him down could not displace his consciousness of the eternal bond that united him with his Father in thought, work, and purpose, in the eternal love and fellowship, joy and glory they shared. Because he said "Father," even here, even now, we may have complete assurance that the Father accepted the curse he bore for us, the forsaking he experienced, and the substitution he offered.

The entire goal of propitiation, springing as it did from the infinitely rich love and mercy of God (Eph. 2:4), was to restore us to God as our Father – with all filial confidence, love, and joy, as well as consecrated service, fellowship, and hope. When he said "Father," he said it for us. He is our Head, our Surety, our Covenant. By saying it, he gave us firm assurance that we are reconciled through his sacrifice. He is our "peace" (Eph. 2:14), and when our Peace moaned "Father," we are at peace. There is no more condemnation because he took our condemnation upon himself.

Then, he said "Forgive them." We cannot do justice to this glorious imperative – for it was an imperious request, the Son's justified demand on the basis of his perfect sacrifice – if we look primarily for a Jewish or Roman fulfillment of this. For whomever the Son seeks forgiveness, forgiveness is granted. Some of the Jews and Romans who crucified him are certainly included. Yet, we must connect this to the "sheep," those whom the Father had given him before the foundation of the world (John 17:11,24), those for whom he laid down his life (John 10:15), his elect, those for whom he undertook to be their surety, their sacrificial lamb. It was for these alone he became the curse, for whom he perished –

else we must say that Jesus petition failed. Coming as it did, at this moment, such a thought is abhorrent. No, everyone included in that petition will be forgiven. In one important sense, we were forgiven at that moment, though the individual bestowal of that forgiveness and resulting peace awaited God's regenerating grace, producing faith and repentance.

And whom did he tell the Father to forgive? Ah, here we reach impenetrable depths of mercy. He did not ask the Father to forgive his friends, for all had forsaken him. He had no friends at that moment. His disciples were in such confusion and despair that we can hardly call them his friends. No, it was his enemies for whom he pled forgiveness. It was for the very miserable sinners whose evil deeds crucified him. Even as he experienced such grief and agony – and only a completely righteous soul and a completely obedient man can ever know the horror of being forsaken by God, of having the sins of others imputed to him, of being cursed for sins not his own, of "becoming sin" – he claimed for us the right of forgiveness. All was done. Satisfaction made. Atonement secured. Everlasting righteousness brought in and sealed. Redemption accomplished.

This "forgive them" – far from being the weak hope of a dying man – was a cry of victory from the depths of human misery and from the heights of divine satisfaction. He knew. He had triumphed. He had secured. Therefore, "Father, forgive them." None who look to him will ever be ashamed or have their sins held against them. By this cry, Jesus Christ hath forever cast our sins in the depths of the sea. They are covered by his blood, drowned in his love, wiped away by his satisfaction.

The last words – "for they know not what they do" – is not an excuse for those actually engaged in crucifying him. It is not an excuse for us. Jesus does not plead our forgiveness on the basis of our ignorance. How could he who said, "If I had not done among them the works which none other man did, they had not had sin: but now have they both seen and hated both me and my Father" (John 15:24), indict his own person and work by claiming that they were ignorant of who he really was and what he came to do? This would be a blatant contradiction and a denial of the clarity of him who was "the light of the world." Yet, in another important sense, our sins are evidence of a deep-seated, willful, and antagonistic blindness to God's claims upon our lives. Our ignorance is culpable.

It is an ignorance that has engulfed us in utter helplessness. All the schooling in the world cannot free a man from his furious pursuit of self-justification for the alienation he feels in his heart and mind. Thus, our Lord is having pity upon us by his statement. It is as if he had said, "They do not know what they are doing, for they have blinded themselves, and they are unable to do anything about their condition. They cannot but reject me. Forgive them, Father."

Such undeserved pity – do we deserve pity? No, we have suppressed the truth in unrighteousness (Rom. 1:18-19). We went astray from the womb speaking lies and believing them – about ourselves, about God, about the world in which we live. We have done all we could to flee from him and his claims upon us. Our willful blindness brought him to the cross. Rather than holding even this against us, he pleads that the Father might forgive us, his crucifiers. He prays that our eyes might be opened to who he is, that though we have no claim upon the Father's mercy, that he might nonetheless extend it to us for the sake of the Son – the very One whom our blindness rejected and slew.

In a world of divisions and prejudices at every social, political, and philosophical level, we do well to remember our Savior's words. If judgment and wrath were not his final words at the cross, they should not be ours in life. Yes, there will be a final judgment; the wrath of God will abide forever upon those who reject the Son (John 3:36). Yes, we must judge in terms of the truth of God's word (John 7:24). Since the Son of God forgave us, however, his malevolent, sin-blinded tormentors, we ought to forgive others. We must point our fellow-crucifiers to the One who forgives, that through him they too might obtain mercy!

And mercy shall prevail – not at the expense of divine justice but because the Lamb of God bore God's judgment. The gospel of mercy and grace is not sentimentalism but blood-purchased security, not hedonistic love but justice-satisfying love, not smooth words of therapy but of saving power forged before the altar of divine justice. It did not spring from moral relativism or lowering of God's just claims but from the strictest conformity to divine righteousness. This is the great hope of the world: that there is legitimate forgiveness from the Judge of all the earth because there was full and specific atonement made at the cross. Let us revel in forgiveness, in mercy so deep that it actually obtained our redemption, in love so efficacious that it celebrated its success and claimed its rights at the very moment of its deepest sacrifice.

How we must love him! How each fiber of our being must thrill to his "Father, forgive them!" How secure we are in his wondrous love! Having loved his own, he loved them to the end (John 13:1). Can we not love him? Do we not tremble before such love? Does it not satisfy us above all other loves, heal every wound, and calm every agitation of conscience? Can we not give ourselves to loving him in return, a love that must be like his because it is joined to his love in a living union of grace and glory? This love will seek him, obey him, and delight in him above all else (John 14:15). All his blood-stained garments smell of myrrh and cassia to the sin-wearied soul. Truly, whom do we have in heaven beside him and whom do we desire on earth beyond him? Everything we shall ever after receive flows from his love command: "Father, forgive them." May his love be the banner of our lives!

And when we interact with others, should not a love like his be behind all our words, even words of warning? Should not there be a constant underlying sense of having received such mercy, so that we are merciful and charitable to others, even to our enemies? We are to forgive our enemies, love our persecutors, pray for them, and seek to do them good. How? Why? Because this is the way the Son of God saved us, and his love, as we begin to understand something of its magnificence by the power of the Holy Spirit, is the way we are filled with the fullness of God.

Yet, we respond, others are blind to their sins. They are enemies of God and deserve what they get. So were we. They are wedded to perversity, statism, and self. We crucified the Lord of glory. They are utterly unworthy of being forgiven, being enemies of God and builders of the city of man. Fire should come down and consume them. To say this condemns us, for we were all these things. Yet, he forgave us, and the flow of history from those glorious words to the very end will be the triumph of God's mercy in Christ over man's willful ignorance, blindness, and rebellion.

If You Love Me

There came a day, even a moment, when being a Christian took on new urgency joined with empowering freshness. Perhaps it occurred progressively, which is likely, for the Spirit's witness to Jesus, his communication of the Prince of life as our food and drink usually unfolds and possesses each soul little by little. No new revelation came beaming from heaven; nothing beyond the same old Bible, the old Bible new. Obligatory discipleship, necessary duty became a "you have come to Mount Zion," the delight of the soul, a straight and level path, a lighter burden.

Sin was still present, as were the circumstances and pressures of life. There is no Jesus without the cross. Yet, he suddenly became a living and breathing reality, transcendently glorious, joyfully near, unspeakably satisfying. No greater pleasure was sought or needed than to enjoy his promised presence, his covenant advocacy before the throne of God. You heard his living voice, inviting you to enjoy his redemption and reconciliation, securing each day's mercy and faithfulness by his worthiness, his headship more than an idea but fullness received by faith, grace upon grace.

Then came the reading in John's Gospel: "If you love me, keep my commandments" (John 14:15). Guilt too often focused upon the second half of this line. Yes, to keep his commandments is my duty. Can I? I tried often. Or had I tried? Had I kept them enough? Can the second half ever be without the first? Perhaps for a while there may be an attempt to keep some or all. But there is not much joy in it. There is less power and virtually no consistency. The sirens of the flesh call out not to take obedience too seriously. Obey maybe in a few things. Keep some areas for yourself, some thoughts, a few hours, some seemingly trifling indulgences for self. Then, the predicted fall occurs. There is pride again. Anger rears its ugly head. Self fights to dethrone the Crucified. What a bloody sword is my tongue! The guilt follows. Another sermon on some neglected duty. I am tired and frustrated now, again.

What did the first half say? "If you love me." Wait. Is Jesus placing obedience on an entirely different plane? He is not calling me to performance piety. There is nothing here about tradition, or merit, or karma. Love. Love for him. Love is personal. It suggests a relationship, a commitment, a whole-soul, emotional, warm movement toward him as a person, the Person, the one who loved me first. Oh, the cross! The realization dawns that obedience is personal, to a person, to the Savior whose every word and action drips love and sacrifice, submission to the Father because he loves the Father, as a Son should his father, as only the Son does. I return to consider the cross.

Scripture is comparatively silent on its gore and pain, not at all like cinematic depictions, for we require not the sight but the word, not dazzled eyes but believing hearts. Leading up to that bloody hill, there is the horrible night in the garden. Will he take the cup? He prays, if possible, for it to pass. The thought of the cup is perfect holiness and pure love unhinged before the thought of becoming sin and bearing curse. All its horrors are presented. Not the horrors of hell, mind you – how could the Creator of hell be afraid of hell? Fire: he made it. Death: do you not remember Lazarus? Death obeys him. No, the horrors of something far worse than death and hell commonly considered. The cup is the apprehension of divine justice poised to exact its full toll. It is the sword being drawn, ready to strike him down, he who is holiness and love itself in word and deed.

Two loves drained the cup that night. Two loves bore the cursed cross. The first was his love for his Father. "I always do those things that please him" (John 8:29). "My meat is to do the will of him that sent me, and to finish his work" (John 4:34). Why? I and my Father are one – in existence, will, and love. Before there was anything, I was daily his delight, rejoicing always before him (Prov. 8:30). The Father loves me; he has committed everything into my hand. I love him. I came because I love him, willingly submitted to his will in my agreed upon work as Mediator. Yes, I learned obedience through the things I suffered, but it was love for the Father that sanctified the suffering. It was love that taught me, in the days of my flesh, to pray, even in the garden: "Thy will be done." This is love and devotion uniting in a holy fervor and active pursuit of the Father's will – the cross. It is my ultimate expression of absolute devotion to my Father, of my oneness with him, love for him, and submission to him.

And the other love? For us, this is something uncomfortably amazing to contemplate, for no one has or can love us like this. At God's appointment, "love" is the human word used, but great care must be exercised when we use it. On peril of blasphemy and the basest ingratitude punished in the lowest hell, we best not say or act in any way, in any relationship, that trivializes a word defined by the sacrifice of the Son of God. He loves us. Even in the garden, he commanded, commanded, mind you, the malevolent soldiers to "let these go" (John 18:8). Of all whom the Father has given me, I will lose none; not even in this Satan's hour, never. When my love is set, it never fails of its purpose. I love you. My love will accomplish its goal. I will die for you. I will take this sword into my own holy heart. I will be the appointed substitute, surety, propitiation, and curse. I will be the sacrifice, the priest, and the altar. I will drink this cup for my sheep, for I know them by name, and each bitter drop is for them. They are all written in my book. If I must stare at all my bones, if I must be forsaken, if I must become the burnt offering, I will love you.

Now, if you love me. Do you? How often have you returned to these scenes of love, lingering for just an hour with me in prayer, even for your own soul? Have you thought recently upon my sacrifice? Have you considered me? Do the chords of your redeemed heart no longer tremble when they think on Calvary, where love and mercy kissed holiness and satisfied justice? Do you ever think that I am now at the Father's right hand – yes, removed from you physically, I know, but I will soon be restored to you, my beloved – interceding for you, opening heaven's gates to you by my sacrifice of love, by the merit of my love, by the righteousness of my love?

What would-be loves are weakening your love for me? Judas may have hanged himself, but his kiss of treachery lingers on in every word, action, and relationship that hides my love behind the cloud of self, willfulness, and forgetfulness. Here I am. Love me. Pray, as I did, not to enter into any temptation that will diminish my love, make it common, or just another love among the world's many attempts to fill the miserable void left by sin. Will you not watch with me? Just one hour. I wrote to you to "look unto Jesus, the author and finisher of your faith" (Heb. 12:2). I invite you to revel, tremble, rejoice, and triumph in my love.

What will you not give up to love me? I have done all for you. Do your taste buds need changing, so that you will lose your appetite for sin? Do you still find that the world's worries and pressures are so burdensome that you often feel like collapsing in a heap of despair? Do you fill your life with a swirl of constant activity, so much so that I am an afterthought? Where are you bleating in the darkness of fear, my sheep? Where are you eating at the trough of sin that can no longer satisfy you if you have tasted but a crumb of my love? Here I am. I love you. I am your light, your bread, your water, your resurrection, your door, your way, truth, and life. I am all you have been created and re-created to enjoy. Love me. Do you?

You are my friends, yes, friends, for all things that the Father has told me I have made known to you, if you do what I say – because you love me. I am preparing a place where we can love, rejoice, and laugh together. Will you give yourself to me? Whatever your past, I make all things new. Whatever your sins, my blood has satisfied the claims of my Father and your Father. Whatever your present temptations, I am with you. Be of good cheer; I love you. Resist the devil, because you love me, and he will flee from you.

You see, my love saved the world. It destroyed the evil one and cast him out of heaven. It saved you. It saves you. It will save you. If you love me, then, keep my commandments. My word, which is the will of my Father, will be your delight and meat as it is mine. Obedience will be your privilege as a son and daughter, as a disciple, as a lover of me. It will be your delight. Are you weak? I will strengthen you. Are you weary? I will carry you. Are you fearful? Distracted? Doubting? Behold my hands and side. Let no other love intrude.

~3~

Exalted, Extolled, and Very High: The Lord of Glory in his Kingdom

Kingdom Sayings

Most Americans live in or near "edge cities," large scale commercial, specialty retail, and restaurant developments standing outside but in close proximity to traditional urban centers. These centers grow rapidly, tangibly before our eyes. They swallow up land and alter the landscape, tend to be homogenous in their appearance and offerings, and attract large numbers of people who live, work, and shop nearby. Some have made these edge cities the model for Christ's church and kingdom: build it big, make a "splash," offer countless amenities, appeal to the broadest possible number, and avoid as many distasteful truths as possible. In this, they grossly neglect our Lord's more startling declarations concerning the nature of his church and kingdom.

In Luke 12:32, he says, "Fear not, little flock; for it is your Father's good pleasure to give you the kingdom." The context in which he says this is remarkable. In the previous verses he has forbidden his disciples to make the pursuit of food, drink, and clothing, i.e., material possessions and security, the primary objective of their lives. Immediately after, he says to "sell what you have and give alms" (v. 33). He is telling us that his kingdom is a gracious gift of God. It consists not of material prosperity and outward pomp but of self-denial and sacrifice. His kingdom is decidedly not the "build it and they will come" mentality. It is quite the opposite of the "God wants you prosperous" non-gospel and "find your purpose in life" pseudo-gospel promoted by false teachers. God's kingdom originates in his gift to sinners, requires faith, not presumption, and leads to self-sacrifice rather than self-promotion.

Later in Luke (17:20), Jesus states that his kingdom does not come with observation. It is not measurable, visible, or predictable by human standard of sight and judgment. It grows imperceptibly, like the grass. He adds, "It is within you." His kingdom manifests itself fundamentally in his saved and being sanctified people, not buildings, political parties, or Christian organizations. God's kingdom rules over these entities and may be promoted by them, but his kingdom does not depend upon them and is not tied to the rise and fall of earthly institutions. Edge cities grow visibly, brick by brick. We watch new stores and office complexes being constructed. We eat at the new restaurants. But God's kingdom is not measured by external phenomena but upon the life-giving and sustaining work of the Spirit in God's people, his Church, Christ's body. We must, therefore, be very careful in both our kingdom expectations and our kingdom methodologies.

It is relatively easy to construct new buildings, set up a web page, or develop Christian "ministries." But to the degree that these emphasize the external marks of human success, i.e., numbers, prosperity, notoriety, to that degree they are in danger of ignoring the true evidence of the presence and power of Christ's kingdom – men and women who are living consecrated and obedient lives to Jesus Christ. His kingdom is not a matter of mere words but of power – divine power, transforming power, progressively unfolding power. This cannot be measured by worldly standards, on graphs, by church-growth models. The Spirit moves when and how he pleases, and we cannot control him. Jesus encourages vigorous kingdom effort, but he would have us reject the temptation to measure kingdom growth by the world's standards of success.

In Matthew 13:31-33 Jesus compares the growth of his kingdom to the mustard seed and to leaven. They have this in common – they are small and spread imperceptibly to the sight and judgment of men. They spread, but it is slow and steady. Fast growing trees are notoriously shallow in the root and weak in the trunk, like the "yuppie tree," the Bradford Pear. Developers love them because they grow quickly; homeowners learn to hate them because they are prone to disease and cannot withstand winds and storms. How sadly appropriate that the yuppie mentality yields weak trees!

This parable opposes the modern "get spiritually rich quick" Christian mentality and the "five-points-to-cure-your-life" sermon. These are diseases that fight against true sanctification, which deepens through cross-bearing, progresses as much or more through adversity as prosperity, and, given our weakness, is usually slow. But slow growth is best. Oaks are stronger than pines; their slow growth yields deeper roots and stronger cores. But note that both leaven and mustard seeds grow. They eventually reach maturity.

Our kingdom expectations and efforts must consider the "later" as much or more than the "now." Kingdom-builders are seed spreaders and leavening agents. They should not expect immediate results, though sometimes God does in his providence accelerate his work. Growth comes through faithfulness and patience. Growth may come later in our lives, in the next generation, or in the case of many of the church fathers and reformers, several generations later. This is not cause for frustration but for greater diligence, for we labor with the confidence that our efforts are not in vain. One sows and another reaps (John 4:37). The kingdom of Jesus Christ will spread and fill the world. God's word will not return to him without accomplishing his purposes for sending it. Mercy sown and shown in Jesus' name to the world's poor and needy will yield a rich gospel harvest and obtain our Savior's approbation (Matt. 10:42).

The power of all legitimate kingdom efforts is the word. Jesus preached the "word of the kingdom" (Matthew 13:19). A frequently recurring title for gospel preaching is the "preaching of the kingdom" (Matthew 9:35; Acts 20:25; 28:31). Gospel preaching and the kingdom are inseparable. When God's word is faithfully proclaimed as the grace of God that has appeared through Jesus Christ, in its breadth and depth, confronting and calling men, the kingdom is proclaimed; its power is exerted. Jesus unsheathes the sharp two-edged sword that proceeds from his mouth and gives life to the believing and judgment to the unbelieving (Isaiah 49:2; 2 Corinthians 2:16; Revelation 1:16; 19:15).

The failure to take seriously the centrality of preaching in the plan of God to build the kingdom of his Son is evidenced in a variety of ways, always with devastating results. There has rarely been as much "kingdom activity" with such small, lasting "kingdom results." Why is this? Why do more preachers compromise with the present zeitgeist rather than resist it? Why have this and previous generations spent without replenishing the spiritual capital bequeathed by their ancestors? Why do many lack the purity resolve of Joseph, especially when we have God's full word, a much fuller measure of the Holy Spirit, and a full entrance to heaven through the intercession of our Savior? We have departed from the word – and thus we have separated ourselves from Christ's kingdom power. God has wonderfully united the reading, preaching, explanation, application, and practice of his word with the power of his kingdom. He thereby emphasizes his sovereign grace and power, tests our personal submission, disciplines our stubbornness, and confronts our pride.

The hope for the broader church in our nation is that it will hear again the voice of our Savior. He calls us away from personally constructed edge cities of convenience and programs to the lasting city which has as its enduring foundation his holy word. By application, every congregation of believers, large and small, should endeavor to be a thriving center of expository preaching and discipleship. Christian political efforts should be based upon the word rather than "playing the game" compromise. And preaching, the lack of which is the crisis of the West, should be systematic, confrontational, encouraging, motivating, not because the preacher has mastered the art but because the Spirit honors and works through the simple proclamation of the word of the kingdom, the Bible, in all its authority, majesty, and power.

Before Pilate, our Savoir made one of his most remarkable kingdom sayings. "My kingdom is not of this world." Pilate may have been driven mad by this statement. His entire worldview was suddenly exposed as nothing but a house of cards. Like most men today, Pilate only knew of one sort of kingdom – the rule of autonomous man exerted through the machinery of political power and directed according to the whims of those with luck enough to possess it. Suddenly, Pilate stood naked, his paradigm exposed as a sham, an attempt to escape from the only true and lasting kingdom.

Pilate is not the only one who has experienced frustration and perplexity at the words of our Savior. They remain jarring. There is another kingdom, the real kingdom, which is not of this world. Its origin is in the mind and will of the Creator of this world. It depends not upon the power of man, his institutions and laws, but upon God's Spirit (Zech. 4:6). It is the rule he unceasingly exerts over this world, everyone and everything in it. It is the rule he has given to his Son as our Mediator, as a reward for his obedience and suffering. Neither Roman pluralism nor American secularism can do anything against this kingdom. All their efforts to oppose it will actually serve God's purpose to confound the wisdom of this world and build the kingdom and Church of his Son.

Whatever blind men are doing, the kingdom of God has its seat in heaven, at the right hand of the Eternal, Sovereign, and Omnipotent God, where the crucified Lord of glory now sits clothed with all authority and power to bring the blessings of his reign to all who believe his promises and turn from the world's kingdom. Submit to him and be blessed. Believe in him and be saved. Labor for him and be rewarded. Walk with him and have joy unspeakable. Fail to do any one of these things, and no edge city on the planet, secular or religious, can help or satisfy you. Do them, and the Son of righteousness, the only King, will arise with healing on his wings.

The Glorious Lamb

In the opening chapter of John's Revelation, the reader finds him in exile on Patmos, most likely in the wake of the crackdown against the church under the reign of Nero. Alone, possibly discouraged, and undoubtedly concerned for the churches bereft of their apostle, John is given the answer to the political and religious turmoil of his day. It is not a political answer, though it has political ramifications. It is not a "we need more conferences and programs" answer, though it is certainly energizing. It is certainly not a "we need to find a way to make friends, achieve consensus, and be relevant" answer, though it is the most vital and relevant message on earth. The answer is the revelation of the Lamb of God. He is ruling over the affairs of men, present and building his Church, and empowering his people to hold fast to his gospel in the midst of oppression and persecution.

John is first. The beloved disciple who reclined upon the breast of Jesus is confronted with the exalted Savior. He is no longer lowly; he is now "exalted, extolled, and very high" (Isa. 52:13). Having suffered and died, he is the glorified Lamb, ruling at the right hand of the Father, crowned with glory and honor. The glorious Lamb is the revelation of Revelation. His is the kingdom and power. John needed this confirmation and encouragement. Seeing the Savior in his glory immediately brought John back to where Thomas had been over three decades earlier: on his face, worshipping, enraptured with love, filled with awe. Everything John wrote in the remainder of this book is an extension of this initial vision. No power on earth, not the Antichrist or the Beast, can stand before the juggernaut of his power, the brilliance of his glory, and the march of his reign.

And this Lamb walks among the candlesticks, the Church. This is the message those struggling believers needed more than anything else in the world. This revelation was also for John; he needed to remember that his personal presence was not required to safeguard and direct Christ's lambs. The one with eyes like flames of fire and feet like polished brass – he is the one who is constantly present in his Church, protecting his people against their enemies, guiding them through his word and Spirit, and strengthening them by his abundant grace. The church needed this reminder. She is not a "concerned citizens group," a social gathering place, a religious assembly. She is the lighthouse of the Lamb, who fills her with his glory, illumines her in dark places, and enables her to shine the light of the knowledge of his glory to the farthest reaches of the globe. Because the glorious Lamb walks in the midst of the Church, she has life and light, understanding, and strength. Her light shines from the throne of God, and its brilliance cannot be extinguished. Her foes cannot snuff it out, however hard they may try. Jesus is always with his Bride by the seven-fold Spirit who burns before the throne of God, a metaphor emphasizing his limitless resources and power.

As the remainder of the book unfolds, it is clear that the glorious Lamb is not a spiritual power that makes those who love him feel better or soar untouched above very earthly crises. He is not the crutch of the weak, the psychologist of the depressed, or the hope of fools. He is and does two primary things according to John's multi-layered vision; he chastens, encourages, and empowers his Church, and he destroys his enemies. With respect to the former, we might do well to remember that Jesus cannot be domesticated. He speaks with penetrating conviction to the unfaithful churches, those seeking détente with the world, those who lost their first love, and those unwilling to stand for truth regardless of personal cost. He calls these "Jezebels," i.e., whores. They are unfaithful to their husband; repentance alone will save them from the wrath of the Lamb. His words of encouragement to the faithful who did not deny his name in the midst of persecution are some of the most precious, tender, and powerful words recorded in the Bible. They will reign with him. He will feed them. He will clothe them. Here is a King of incomparable compassion speaking life-giving words of power to give what he promises.

For his enemies, whose judgment comprises the bulk of the book, their case is hopeless. Natural disaster, foreign armies, internal squabbles, and divine intervention – each of these is a thunderbolt of judgment in his hand. He is the sovereign Lord of heaven and earth; he is coming upon the clouds to destroy the

Harlot (Jerusalem) and the Beast (Rome). They have dared to reject his gospel and persecute his Bride. And their ring leader, the devil, he too will feel the wrath of the Lamb, and his history is one of progressive defeat leading to final judgment. The staff of his power has been broken by the resurrection and enthronement of the glorious Lamb.

The bloody Warrior of Revelation is a shocking sight to those of us who lived too long under the fog of the "please let Jesus save you" Jesus. It is no wonder that liberal scholars want to expunge this book from the hubristic "scholar's canon" of the New Testament. In their hearts, they too are harlots and beasts, who know too well that if this Jesus really exists – and they are none too sure of their learned denials – then their doom is also sealed. For the glorious Lamb brooks no rivals. The day of his wrath is come, and who is able to stand before his vengeance?

We also desperately need to recover this vision of the glorious Lamb. We have two choices: surrender to him in faith and love, as John did, or reject him and face the fate of Jezebel. Every true church must bow before the reigning Lamb with mystery, wonder, awe, and love! Do we know and see him reigning in glory, present in power by his Spirit? Do our hearts burn within us when he opens his word to us? And where are those who respond to the crises of our times with the message of Revelation? Not the response of fearful resignation, "Well, I told you things would get bad for the church," but the beloved disciple's response, "The enemies of the Lamb's church are doomed."

Jesus has not changed. The glory and power of the Lamb are undiminished. He still offers comfort to the afflicted, power to the weak, hope to the despairing. He reigns. He has lost none of his freshness, his conquering determination, or his sustaining power. What is our present national situation if not an indication that his wrath has fallen upon us? What is our present church situation if not an indication that he has thrown the Jezebels of liberalism and compromise into the prostitute's bed of disease and weakness? Trifle with this King, play games with his gospel, fleece his flock, and you will be the object of his fury. Love his gospel, love him more than life, love him as the glorious Lamb of God, and he will unveil his light and unleash his power for your deliverance.

This is the choice facing the present-day church. The sides are formed. This is also the choice facing the nations. The sides have formed. Secularism is nothing but the resurrection of worn-out statism. Celebrityism is nothing but the Roman Circus rebuilt. He has crushed these enemies before. His garments are already bloodied from these contests; he is lifting up the head at the brook, fresh from his former victories, looking for new enemies to conquer. Rome is a museum. First-century Jerusalem is under seven layers of rubble. Jesus walks in the Church and marches through history. Make the choice to fall before him as a dead man, like John did. All the problems of your life will not immediately disappear, and our foes are not likely to tuck tail and run tomorrow. But the King is on the move. His foes are scared to death without knowing exactly the cause of their fear. They are filled with fury against the Lamb and his followers. Let us give them something to hate and fear – changed lives, bold proclamation, kingdom prayer, love for the Savior, no trembling before their threats. Their boiling wrath directed at the church is an indication of the fiery wrath of the Lamb lit beneath their feet. We have nothing to fear from them but must only fear and adore him.

From Now On

Given the present distractedness of the Church, several generations of antinomianism, and the desire for relevance at all costs, it was inevitable that we would fall into the abyss of consumerism's pursuit of convenience, easy spirituality, and less responsibility. It is one thing to have Saturday evening services so that families can catch "church" on the way home from the mall and have all day Sunday for other activities.

It something else entirely when we reduce the Christian life to a series of manageable principles, when Christian lifestyle stores market the latest Jesus accessories, when study Bibles resemble glossy magazines, when it is no longer possible in most worship services to "be still and know that I am God" because the music is deafening. When these things happen, the devolution has reached a level where a momentary pause is recommended. Are we willing to sacrifice mature Christian discipleship upon the altar of convenience and consumerism? Are sight and sound a substitute for faith and love? Do we really believe Jesus, the Head of the Church, applauds our efforts to fit his kingdom in with our other interests and pursuits, to turn his gospel into a New Age philosophy of self-improvement? Or would he drive the money-changers from our electronic temples of mammon?

Against these things, I would urge that we take seriously the all-consuming nature of Christ's kingdom. Consider Paul's teaching in 1 Corinthians 7. Here he addresses questions raised by the Corinthians about sexuality, marriage, and singlehood. They were extremely divided by these questions, unable to find the biblical balance between genuine piety and ascetic escapism. Some were advocating the moral superiority of celibacy, even within marriage. Others were suggesting that believers should divorce unbelieving spouses in order to serve Christ more devotedly. Paul systematically refutes their false piety, their ascetic dualism between the material and spiritual, and their belief that the kingdom of Jesus Christ renders obsolete the authority structures God instituted at creation. Along the way, he makes one of the profoundest series of statements to be found in his letters.

He says "the time is short" (v. 29). This is not a declaration of the any-moment-return of Jesus, a belief Paul did not have. The phrase is more accurately translated, "The times have been drawn together." The noun he uses for "time" is not the Greek word for quantity of time but for quality of time. In other words, this time period is defined by that which has forever changed and redirected time, the entrance into the world of Christ's kingdom. However long this period lasts, and Paul makes no attempt in his letters to quantify it, it is short. The entire period has been compressed; every moment is defined by his kingdom, its inauguration, progress, and consummation. It must be spent in the light of Christ's kingdom, his reign over all things, and his work in the world. Hence, each generation of the Church must live in the constant light of this kingdom, its priorities and perspectives, like Christ's wise virgins, with their lamps always burning, always ready for the Bridegroom's return. Not only is each generation given a relatively short time to develop and defend the kingdom of Christ, but that time must also be used intensively.

Then he says, "From now on." This phrase makes the "present distress" (v. 26) more than a local issue in Corinth: imminent persecution, congregational upheaval, the A.D. 49 famine. "From now on" makes it clear that the "distress" and the "drawing together of the times" must make a permanent change in our outlook on life. Hence, as he immediately adds, issues of marriage, mourning and rejoicing, buying and selling, and each believer's life in the world, draw their significance from the kingdom of Jesus Christ. They are not ends in themselves. Each is secondary to the issue of Christ's kingdom.

If I am married, it is so that I might pursue the kingdom of Christ with the specific gifts he has given me. If I am single, it is not a time to pine away, waiting for "real life" to begin, but a period of life in which to pursue pleasing the Lord with undivided focus, without the responsibilities and troubles of married life. Paul ultimately answers the Corinthians' letter by directing them to something higher, more defining, and vastly more important than their questions about sex, family, and singlehood. He directs them to consider the times in which they live, that the kingdom of Christ has now been established upon the foundations of his glorious person and saving work, that life must be lived in the light of his reign.

"From now on" applies to us as much as to the Corinthians. In this period, we will have distress and face tension in living for Christ. Married believers face the troubles and responsibilities associated with this relationship – mainly divided attention between domestic needs and kingdom responsibilities. Fathers face this tension in raising, guiding, and providing for their unmarried daughters. All believers face this distress in coping with sin, trying to stand for Jesus Christ in a fallen world, and endeavoring to maintain the balance of living in the world faithfully without being of the world. Persecuted believers, faithful churches seeking to stand for the whole counsel of God in a culture of sound bites, and men seeking to remain pure in a pornified culture face this distress, this kingdom tension. It is dangerous to seek its alleviation by convenience spirituality, worldly Christianity, and absorption with the present age. Christ came to introduce a sword into our own lives and families, our thinking, and our relationship with the world.

Paul exhorts the Corinthians to enter into this kingdom perspective because "the fashion or form of this world is passing away." "Form" is an old theater word for "mask." The world, the unbelieving portion of mankind with its priorities, affections, and goals, is constantly trying to mask its obsolescence. We might look at it like this. Fashions, car models, and entertainment forms constantly change, each promising to be better than the last, more fulfilling, and more necessary because you are worth it. To these we might add every new philosophy that arises, new political campaign, and new scientific dogma. These have been definitively exposed as futile and are progressively fading away in their significance. What counts is the kingdom of Jesus Christ, that we are seeking it and living in its light, relating to Jesus Christ as our merciful and faithful King, speaking his word, and serving him in all things. If you are not a servant in his kingdom, you will be a slave to irrelevance, easily diverted, constantly distracted, and always frustrated.

The kingdom of Jesus Christ brings tension because it is personally confrontational. What do I value most, Jesus asks me? Have I sold everything for the pearl of great price? Do I view marriage or singlehood, riches or poverty, health or sickness, religious liberty or persecution, as the providentially allotted place in which Jesus Christ has placed me that I might know the power of his reign in my life? Kingdom life cannot be comfortably "fit in" with my other activities as one thing I do among many others. Jesus does not beg to be fit in between football games, movies, and family duties. He comes with power and authority to teach me that everything I do, if it is to have meaning and purpose, must be reoriented around his kingdom agenda. His kingdom is the defining reality. All else is now obsolete. There will be new cars, championship games, and fashions next year – and the next. Their very repetition is a sign of their ultimate irrelevance, for being of this world, they grow old and are destined to be folded up as a garment and put away. Our earthly lives have value and lasting purpose only if they are fit into Christ's great kingdom work, the transformation of every area of life until the "desert blossoms like the rose" and the horses' bells have "holiness to the Lord" written upon them (Isa. 35:1; Zech. 14:20).

How will we live from now on? Christ's kingdom is not convenient, reducible to Christian merchandise, advanced through marketing, or celebrated by carnival worship that lacks the simplicity and spirituality that Christ commands (John 4:24). His kingdom is not noisy, brash, syrupy, slick, or trite. His kingdom brings tension. It daily reminds each disciple how far he yet must travel to arrive at his eternal kingdom, how much sin there remains to be combated, how many souls must yet hear the King's message, and how many areas of life must yet be conformed to his word. It also confronts us that our business, family, sexuality, and enjoyment of God's many gifts are never ends in themselves. They must contribute to the kingdom of Christ, be transformed by his reign, and brought under his authority.

Is his light shining through them? Is the reign of Christ being extended through them? Is the King pleased with us? It matters not if we are pleased with ourselves. Is the King pleased? As we speed through life, rapidly approaching the King's assessment, what will be his judgment upon our lives? "Here lived a selfish man." "Here lies the dust of a man who tried to make the world comfortable with Jesus." "These are the remains of a frustrated man who was always trying to fit Jesus in with other things that he valued more." "This generation compromised." Or "Here lives the testimony of a man who lived for me and my kingdom, who sought to please his Lord in all things." This is the life that will be owned and crowned by the Savior on the last day. This is the life we must live from now on.

The Prayer That Saved History

The amount of information available to us is numbing. It is also distracting, for we can do nothing about the vast majority of it, and it is pointless and paralyzing to cram our heads with data. It seems important but only because our time of personal participation is short. The desire is strong to thrash around, stay informed, and add our thoughts and deeds to the mix. Do not get me wrong. History, past and present, is important. Believing in Jesus does not give us permission to retreat within enclaves of spirituality. We testify and hope in a crucified, resurrected, and reigning Savior – all in history. To give history to the wicked is to consign ourselves to a faith-ghetto.

This is exactly the opposite of "all power is given unto me in heaven and earth, disciple all nations, and teach them all things I have commanded you." Where God has placed us, where he calls us to live and labor, we must be self-consciously committed to our Savior's reign over history, his saving presence in history, and his glorious purposes for history. He was nailed to the cross, walked out of the tomb, and ascended to the Father's right hand to claim history for himself as the Mediator of the covenant.

Yet, we must have perspective. The headlines and programs of the wicked must be understood for what they are: evil men trying to define and dominate history for themselves. What they report, how they report it, and what they would have you do with the report is determined by their governing allegiances, by their head, Satan. Much of what we read and witness from the perspective of unbelievers is Satan's war against the Church. They are not presented in this fashion, but this is what they are. How can we distinguish what is true and important from what is not?

Faith must speak here; Scripture must speak. If we neglect them, we shall either be confusedly immersed in the city of man or vainly attempt to hide ourselves from it. Said another way, synthesis or seclusion; both have been a strong temptation to the people of God. Respecting the former, many believers feel that "history is getting away from us; the old ways will not work." The usual conclusion is to seek common ground with unbelievers –

embrace their science, their worship preferences, and their methods at discovering truth. This consensus obsession turned the Calvinist/Puritan movement into Unitarianism, at least in the North, ate the heart out of much of Old School Presbyterianism through capitulation to Liberalism and Pluralism, and has now engulfed the modern American church with various Emergent-isms in worship, theology, and practice. The lesson here is clear: before you engage in history, you had better understand clearly God's program for history, or unbelievers (Satan) will eat you alive.

Seclusion from history is also wrong, for this is to give away the battlefield without even engaging the enemy. Satan loves many aspects of the monastic movement in history. He also delights in pietistic, sentimental Christianity, though not quite as much, for at least that individual soul, family, and congregation – to the degree that they believe God's word and seek to obey him – are immunized somewhat from his deadlier efforts. Still, seclusion movements eventually succumb to his assaults, either by turning faith so inward that it ceases to be biblical faith, capturing their children, or overwhelming them through historical forces they simply refuse to engage. In other words, surround and destroy – or make historically irrelevant.

In the midst of these thoughts, I turn to our Savior's prayer in John 17. This is the prayer of "his hour" (v. 1). He is about to take the "prince of the world," the murderer of men and of history, by the horns and crush him. He is about to bring about that wondrous promise: "now the kingdoms of this world shall become the kingdoms of our Lord, and of his Christ, and he shall reign forever" (Rev. 11:15). He is about to deal with the central issue of history, the reason it looks as it does, with so much misery, tyranny, destruction, and brokenness – sin and rebellion against God. He is about to offer the most necessary sacrifice in history, to take upon himself the sword of God's justice that hangs over man and his history. What does he say at this hour about history? What are his purposes for history? His prayer defines and guides our historical expectations, methods, and engagement.

Glory (vv. 1-5) The goal of history is the manifestation of the glory of God in Jesus Christ. Our Savior's claim upon human history is heavenly; it is comprehensive. No institution, movement, or method that is not self-consciously aimed at the glory of God in the face of Jesus Christ can positively contribute to this goal. It may do so negatively or unwittingly, for God has judged all humanism definitely in his Son. He will judge it. Eternal life is never gained by man's Babels but through faith in Jesus Christ. Glory requires redemption. Jesus finished the work the Father gave him to do. History is saved only through redemption in him. This is the Church's great confession, the confession that makes it most relevant and brings upon her the world's (and Satan's) deepest hatred – man is recovered to heaven, to glory, to history only through the God-man who was crucified in history and did the will of God in history. This will be realized, for the Son has asked his Father for this. His Father never tells him no.

Word (vv. 6-10) The manifestation of God's glory in history and his warfare in history are carried on primarily through his word. This is the original and abiding point of contention: God's word or Satan's; faith or skepticism; life or death. Jesus Christ alone reveals the word God to man in history because he came into history as the God-man. He alone reveals the Father (John 1:14-18). His people are those who keep his word – in everything (John 8:32). There is no such thing as a division between "spiritual" and "historical." Jesus has power over "all flesh," as well as all authority. We must live by every word that has come from God's mouth, proclaiming his word everywhere, backing down from his royal claims in nothing. Jesus is praying for his glory to be manifested through the word. If we turn from the word, we turn from glory – and from history.

Keeping (vv. 11-16) Jesus Christ, God's only Begotten and Beloved, is praying that his people – who keep his word – may be preserved from evil. He does not pray that we shall be taken out of the world. His glory will be revealed in the world, through his faithful people keeping his word in the world. They will do so against all the assaults of unbelieving science, governments, persecution, and media – because he is praying for us. His availing intercession is our salvation and security (Luke 22:32; Heb. 7:25). In its hopefulness and power, you will be able to keep Christ's word and have his joy fulfilled in you, even as he kept his Father's word and remained in his love.

Holiness (vv. 17-19) Our Savior's prayer and program for history is to gather to himself a holy people, zealous for good works. He humbled himself to be sanctified – though he was holiness itself – even though he was the Son, he learned obedience through the things he suffered. Everything that contributes to the holiness of the church – her purity in doctrine, practice, worship – Jesus is praying for these blessings. He secures them for us, not by plucking us out of history but by sanctifying us in it.

Unity (vv. 20-24) Jesus is praying for his Church to be unified in the truth. True unity in heart and mind among us depends upon common submission to the authority of God's word. Jesus is praying for this. It will happen. History will not reveal the progressive unfolding of the church's fragmentation but of its closer agreement in the truth of God. This will lead to the world believing that Jesus is the Christ sent by the Father to save the world.

Glory Coming (vv. 25-26) Jesus is praying that his whole church will be with him. What glory this is! He wants us to behold his glory, even share in his mediatorial glory as the Son of man. There is a reward for faithfulness – to be with Jesus, our Lord and Savior. This is also faith's supreme motivation – to behold firsthand the glory of God in the face of Jesus Christ. We need not compromise with worldlings nor flee from them in order to realize glory; we need but be faithful to what God has promised and what his Son has prayed – and is praying. Deny future glory, deny future hell, and you turn from history.

This prayer saved history. It is saving history. We must believe and pray it: with faith and tears, hope and joy. Our labors and reading of history must be completely dominated and shaped by it. Jesus' prayer for his Church is the most important thing occurring in human history at this moment. His prayer is also our only source of wisdom and strength to engage where our Savior is engaging: keeping God's word, seeking unity in the truth, praying for the gathering of the church into Christ. His prayer is guiding history. It reveals God's purpose and plan for history. Relevance is found, hope dawns, when by faith we hear our Savior's prayer, believe that the Father will hear him, and devote our lives to the fulfillment of what he has asked from his Father. The Father will do it. He loves his Son. His Son loves us. This love is our joy and strength. It is our historical hope, identity, and marching orders. The glory of God in the face of Jesus Christ will prevail over all the chaos and blindness around us.

Prince of Peace

I was recently asked by a relative, "How can you say that Jesus Christ is the King when there is so much trouble in the world?" I paused for a moment. It does seem rather strange that one of his royal titles is "Prince of Peace." The world is always at war. I read recently that since 1789 our nation has known only twenty years without war of some kind. Is "Prince of Peace" merely an honorary title? Perhaps it refers to the spiritual realm and has nothing to do with the "real world." Or maybe his peace is reserved for the Jewish millennium of popular lore.

I say "lore," for Premillennial eschatology and especially its Dispensational version cannot be sustained exegetically, theologically, or historically. It contradicts our Savior's "ought not the Christ to have suffered and enter into his glory" (Luke 24:26)? He had suffered; he has entered into his glory. What glory? The kingdom of glory promised to him as a reward for his obedience, suffering, and death (Ps. 2:7-8; Isa. 53:11-12; Dan. 2:44; 7:13-14; Phil. 2:8-11). Peter states that the death and resurrection of Jesus Christ are his sitting on David's throne. He is not a "King in waiting" but is now "Lord and Christ" (Acts 2:30-36). John speaks of him as the "Prince of the kings of the earth" (Rev. 1:5) and Paul as "King of kings and Lord of lords" (1 Tim. 6:15).

There is no place for a historical gap between his ascension and his reign. His ascension was his monarchical procession to the right hand of his Father, the rebuilding of David's true tabernacle and sitting on David's throne (Acts 2:30; 15:16-17), and the inauguration of his promised mediatorial reign. He will reign at God's right hand until all his enemies are made a footstool for his feet. Then comes the end (1 Cor. 15:24-25) – his return in glory, the consummation of all things, the resurrection of the just and unjust, and the final judgment.

There is an alternative to this view that depicts his reign in such spiritual terms that little historical manifestations of his kingdom are to be expected. Yes, souls will be saved; many souls. And Jesus Christ is the King in that he generally rules over things so that his sheep are saved and his church preserved. But on this view, our Savior's reign is little concerned with redeeming men in history so that the "desert blossoms like the rose" and the kings of the earth bring their gifts to him (Isa. 35:1; Ps. 72:10). I cannot accept this as a legitimate reading of the prophets (Ps. 72; Isa. 2:2-4; 65:17-25), our Lord's kingdom parables, or the historical declarations pertaining to the increase and manifestations of his kingdom. There is no legitimate way to spiritualize his warnings to kings and judges (Ps. 2:10-12), Jesus' "and hereafter you shall see the Son of man sitting on the right hand of power" (Matt. 26:64), or John's description of the enthroned Savior slaying the beast of Revelation by the sword coming out of his mouth. Statism will be killed by the gospel. Jesus by the sword of his mouth slew the Roman Beast and will continue to slay all Babel builders, until by the brightness of his coming he puts down all remaining rebellion against his reign.

The great commission assumes that Jesus has absolute and active authority over the nations – not just over individual men – and that the gospel will impact the nations. While we must take seriously the difference between Old Testament Israel's geo-political existence and the Church's transnational identity as God's holy nation, a mediatorial reign that is without vast, transformative, historical implications does not take the Son of God's incarnation, death, resurrection, and ascension seriously enough. To limit our Savior's reign to the "hearts of men" cannot explain the boldness of the apostles before the governing authorities, exhaust the prophetic depiction of the growth of Messiah's kingdom, or begin to explain the very earthy depiction of Christ's victory over the beast and dragon in John's Revelation.

So, how are we to understand "Prince of Peace?" A few caveats are necessary before we consider the alarming significance of this title. First, we must never think of peace on earth as a consummated peace. This will not come until the end at his return, after Jesus has put down all rule, authority, and power that are opposed to him (1 Cor. 15:25). Second, the peace that Jesus Christ gives is through righteousness and justice. That is, if men and nations do not submit to his gospel reign, they will not know peace. They will feel the other edge of his two-edged sword – the killing edge (2 Cor. 2:16; Rev. 19:15).

Third, his peace implies warfare for his Church, as well as patient suffering. Remember how he said on that last night, "My peace I give to you" (John 14:27). Peace that night? With Satan stalking and the cross looming? Peace comes through doing the will of God (Ps. 119:165). The peace of Jesus Christ is not the absence of conflict but conviction of the presence and promise and power of God that enables calm resolve in adversity and active engagement for his honor in the world. His is the peace evident in the apostles' bold humility that drove the Sanhedrin to frenzied extremes of persecution – yet the "word of God grew and multiplied." Peace is Paul and Silas in the Philippian jail – singing hymns of praise while they were bleeding from their many stripes. Peace is "God with us," the confidence that we serve the King, that it is a privilege to suffer shame for his name and that he will use that shame to convert or to confound his enemies.

There is another side, an alarming side to the Prince of Peace. He gives peace to his people, but he makes war against his enemies (Rev. 19:11-15). Pay careful attention to the present tense verbs in this passage. His reign from his Father's right hand is active. He judges and makes war. Said another way, he makes war against men and nations that will not submit to him. Because he is the Prince of Peace, the unbelieving world is being shaken by his opposition to its unbelief and wickedness. Its mad schemes to save itself – furious money printing and debasing the currency, militarism and unjust wars, fear-mongering globalism – are the Lamb of God sending his hornets upon his enemies to drive them toward destruction. Unbelief and wickedness such as we see in our own nation – the United States as the world's abortion mill, perversion and smut capital, and center of hostility against all vestiges of the West's Christian past – these would prosper if man was in charge. They are not prospering but sending us down into the pit of hell that is the destiny of every nation that forgets God (Ps. 9:15). Man is not in charge. Jesus Christ is. His blood is too precious for his royal claims to be ignored. The Father has covenanted with his Son as Mediator, and his kingdom pleasures will prosper in his hand (Isa. 53:10).

Here we run into a psychological challenge. In answer to the question put to me, "How can you say that Jesus Christ is reigning?" my simple answer was "because those who reject Jesus Christ are being driven to destruction." It is the opposite of what we might expect. No, if Jesus were reigning, there would be no conflict. Everything would be in its place. The wicked would not exist, be killed, or be saved. Some of this is happening. The King has killed many of his enemies in the past three centuries. Have we forgotten the French Revolution? The Communist Revolution? The Nazi Revolution? The American slaughtering of its next generation? Even the World Wars, as they are called, were among other things God's judgment upon Europe for rejecting the crown rights of Jesus Christ and his graciously sent Reformation.

These are not random events, the vicissitudes of history. They are the King marching, judging, and making war. We see but the shadows of his ways. We cannot always see which "side he is on," so we cannot make absolute historical judgments, but we know that if there is calamity in the city, he has done it (Amos 3:6). He makes war against those who reject his word, chastening his people in the process, and promoting his proximate and ultimate purposes. His purposes take time to ripen, but ripening they are and will. Whatever human conspiracies may or may not be behind past and present events, there is one certainty. The King is on the move. He uses whom he will to advance his purposes. He has absolute authority over heaven and earth (Matt. 28:18). This is our historical certainty, the lens through which we must interpret everything that happens.

In an age that wants to define peace on its autonomous terms, it is a great challenge to accept that what we see going on in the world is being directed by Jesus Christ. But in the midst of what looks to us like great darkness, the gospel is growing, especially in areas long void of light. The sufferers will be those who do not submit to the Lamb, who insist upon building the city of man and ignoring the claims of the King. This means that there is a great discipleship challenge facing us. We must warn men of the wrath

Prince of Peace

of the Lamb. This sounds strange, but it is deeply Scriptural (Ps. 2:12; Col. 1:28; 1 Thess. 1:10; Rev. 6:16; 14:10). He did not come to destroy men's lives, but when his gospel offer is refused, he defends his cross and covenant. Remember that he is not now in his humiliation but in his exaltation.

As his shattering peace progresses, the city of man will suffer one devastating blow after another. The Church shall be besieged and must keep her candles burning and walk in humble obedience. She must weep over her sins and those of the land in which she finds herself. She must do as the apostles did, proclaim another King, one Jesus (Acts 17:7), to whom the kings of the earth must give their allegiance or be slain by the sword coming out of his mouth. This is the only historical inevitability: personal and national blessing through confessing Jesus Christ is Lord, or personal and national oblivion by rejecting Jesus Christ as Lord. Glory of glories, he calls us to march with him, clothed in white, reigning with him as his kingdom of priests, and enduring hardship patiently. He will prevail. He is Lord and Christ. He is the Prince of Peace.

Christ and Liberty

As popularly defined, freedom is not a concept found in the Bible. In fact, the Bible repudiates the notion that men should be able to live as they please without external coercion. It does not equate justice and prosperity with men having their needs and wants met by a paternalistic state. True liberty is the antithesis of political and religious polytheism, with men having the right to choose whatever religious and moral, irreligious and immoral, lifestyle they deem will best promote their individual interests. This or any nations that defines freedom in terms of man's desire to be as God, determining good and evil for himself, makes itself an enemy of God. Confronted with so much bluster about preserving the "American way of life," we do well to remember this. We may think of ourselves as the "land of the free and the home of the brave," and men from other nations may wish to share in our bacchanalia, but moral degradation and prosperity by the printing press should never be equated with liberty and honor.

This is not to say that it has always been like this. Nor is it an embracing of anti-Americanism. It is simply a recognition that all the fundamental planks of a legitimate definition of freedom and the path to preserve it are missing from the American government and political scene. In fact, all the pieces are in place and moving toward statism. The deeper reason for this is that individual citizens no longer have any biblical concept of liberty and justice. Turning from the God of our fathers, many demons have rushed into our collective soul to fill the void left by our national rebellion.

We are a sleeping populace. While many are suffering under a self-inflicted economic juggernaut, comparatively few are concerned about anything beyond their personal economic situation. Most still think that there will be a recovery, a solution to our national ills and divisions, a government initiated and mandated one, of course. Self-absorbed and fearful citizens are easy prey for slick promises and smiling politicians, which take the form of bailouts, heavier taxation, and sweeping government jobs programs.

Then, when one hears calls for a "global solution," especially economically, he may be certain that local control and government will be gladly handed over to find security under the shade of a yet larger federal and possibly world government. He may also be sure that he is hearing an admission of defeat on the part of his own state or national government. Governments give up a portion of their sovereignty to other governments when they feel their stability is uncertain or that the best way to enhance their own power is to consolidate it into yet larger economic and judicial schemes.

By far, however, the greatest evidence of our descent into statism is the spiritual blindness of our people and their leaders, whether liberal or conservative. Men run to government to solve their problems only when unbelief has taken firm root in their souls. Unbelief in what, you ask? When men no longer believe in the providence and sovereignty of God over history, when they reject his word as the sufficient guide and the only reliable standard for men and nations, and when they reject the grace and reign of Jesus Christ, they have already declared a revolution against the living God and his enthroned King. Any social revolutions that follow – and they always have and will – are not a return to God's law but a vain attempt at self-preservation and recasting of the characters that promise to captain the ship of revolution against God into safer waters. Never forget that unbelieve always breeds statism, for above all, unbelief wants to escape from God.

What prophetic word has the Church given in this conflict? Does she any longer have a word to give? For many, the Church has nothing to do with this conflict, for the Bible they read only speaks of spiritual matters. The Christ they follow is a King-in-waiting. The God they serve plays second fiddle to the devil in history, at least until the church can be raptured out of history. As a result, the Church has not sounded a clear trumpet of warning. She is embarrassed by her best human legislator, Moses, whose laws remain largely untried in western history. She has ignored her prophets, whose message still sizzles with warnings against statism and political intrigue with supposed friends. She has turned away somewhat from her apostles, whose confession, "We ought to obey God rather than men," would sweep away our participation in those social programs that seek to replace God's word with man's wisdom and God's promise of provision with man's money machine (Acts 5:29).

In churches where there has been something of a "political awakening" to the lifewide implications of the Bible, it has too often been compromise with whichever political party offered the least resistance to our unwelcome intrusion, the party that is only ninety-percent opposed to God's word and Christ's reign rather than ninety-nine percent. Yet, the problem is far deeper than this. Wholly lacking has been any systematic evaluation of our system itself in the light of Scripture, any recognition of the origin and cost of true liberty, and any cross-centered view of political liberty.

The only men in history who have ever enjoyed political liberty are those who have bowed before the cross of Jesus Christ. Only at the cross are we released from the shackles that are incomparably heavier than any political tyranny. Only at the cross are we given a new nature where we have God's law written on our hearts and are able to serve God with courage and independence that do not degenerate into arrogance and libertinism. Only at the cross does our Father lift up our head to see that the purpose of religious and civil liberty is not to live as we please but to serve our precious Savior with adoring, grateful, and obedient hearts. Only at the cross is our curse consumed and sin's slavery broken through faith in his atoning sacrifice and submission to his reign.

Thus, the cross of Jesus Christ is in every way the only charter of political liberty in the world. All other political stands we take, even when they are necessary to stymie evil and unmask evil doers, both of which are important functions of political involvement and of civil government, will not bring true and lasting liberty. Let us not deceive ourselves on this point. Let us not in our desire to "get involved" and "make a difference" lose sight of the cross as the only sign of liberty in the world. Bring men to Jesus Christ, and they will eventually have civil and religious liberty – because it is the fruit of his reign, because it is a blessing he gives to his faithful and confessing children, because he alone is the rightful King of the nations. All others are usurpers, squatters, builders of the city of man, wolves even if they wear sheep's clothing, satanic diversions to keep us from confessing that "Jesus is Lord" – over you, over me, over this nation, over every living soul on this planet, over the fortunes of men and nations. Only in submission to the Prince of the kings of the earth is there and will there ever be true liberty.

Toward this end, see liberty for what it is: the fruit and blessing of submission to Messiah the Prince. When others complain about government, point them to Jesus Christ. When others look to government, point them to the higher and yet more immediate government of Jesus Christ, for the various crises, judgments, and calamities we are facing as a nation are nothing other than the King afflicting and judging his enemies. When others scratch their heads, utterly perplexed and fearful, speak to them lovingly of the King who died for us. Beseech the King to awaken his Church to her divinely empowered calling and weapons, to defend his own name and kingdom, to bless his gospel. Understand that continued unbelief will breed deeper revolution against God, more statism, more calamity.

As the city of man burns, expect for our Savior to build and defend his church. He will also sift and humble her until she recognizes that her chief glory and historical responsibility is to bear witness to his reign at the Father's right hand. When we confess before all, in high places and low, when our only boast is, "Jesus is Lord," he will cause all the nations to flow into his true Church, topple statism, and bless us with true liberty. When the Son shall make you free, you shall be free indeed. Come quickly, O glorious Son of God and make us free, believing, and blessed under your reign!

When the King Marches to War

The furious march of sin is evident in our land. From mass-murders to seemingly endless foreign wars, court decisions granting legal recognition to sodomite marriages, and executive actions on climate and immigration that are based upon utopian fairy tales and political lawlessness, we are witnessing what happens when a nation turns from the God of its fathers. In our case, these fathers have been dead a long time. It is more like the God of our grandfathers, with seven or eight "greats" prefixed. Still, God has a long memory when it comes to personal and national sins for which there has been no repentance. These sins cast long shadows. The judgment shadows are thickening.

It is tempting to comment on each new crisis, but it is as pointless as recording every gasp of a dying man. Do we gain anything by fretting over every tyranny, perversity, or legislative decree born out of sheer madness? This is not indifference, for we see these things as the strokes of the King; loving him, we fear him. Nothing will stop him from breaking the rebellious in pieces like a potter's vessel (Ps. 2:9; Rev. 2:26-27). He is the King of the nations, and if m0en will not submit themselves to him, they will be judged. His march is often slow and progressive, for he gives his enemies time to repent and his friends opportunity to bear a clear and decisive witness to his glory.

We see and feel his judgments far more than his enemies do, for they are blind. We scream, "Look out! Don't you see what you are doing, what this will mean for the nation in which we live?" They do not see it. In fact, they "love the darkness, for their deeds are evil" (John 3:19). The only remedy for national rebellion and national judgment is national repentance toward God and faith in Jesus Christ. Blind nations, like blind men, receive their sight only by coming penitently before the Healer of the nations.

At one level, we should rejoice in our Savior's just judgments, for it confirms that he marches and makes war. If the world were other than as described in Scripture, men would get away with their crimes and build their utopias without any consequences. But the world is not what blind men say it is; it is what God has created it to be and what he has purposed to make of it through his Son. This gives us great confidence, for the "Judge of all the earth will do right" (Gen. 18:25).

At another level, the consequences of national rebellion are horrifying, and we shall feel them acutely. Consider a generation of legally drugged and sedated boys who cannot understand what is wrong with them, look for escape in fantasies, or lash out in disrespect and sometimes bloody violence. Our girls are fed a conflicting message of liberation from God-ordained authority with a constant barrage of sensuality in dress as the true measure of their worth. We feel daily the crushing weight of a debased currency and shall likely experience a hurricane of political change through legal and illegal immigrants who lack any understanding of our history and who join the ranks of those who think there is a magic printing press in Washington D.C. Perhaps this will not be so different, for millions of American citizens vote in the same way. We are not waiting for judgment as much as we are in the midst of it.

Some of the most dedicated "Save America" conservatives sense that it may not be God's intention to save America but to damn it. "America" as a national, political system, as a hodge-podge of Enlightenment rebellion, commercial idolatry, militaristic statism, and political polytheism, is like Rome of old: a sewer into which all filth flows and worse filth flows out. The blood of many, many millions is on our hands: abortion, unjust wars, approved drugs that knowingly harm and kill men but greatly enrich the companies that produce them, and a food supply contaminated with chemicals that most of the civilized world has outlawed. God does not wink at these atrocities. "Change" every four or eight years is not like going to a popish confessional at which men deceive themselves that their slate is wiped clean. This is fool's talk and a fool's dream. "The wicked shall be turned into hell, and all the nations that forget God" (Ps. 9:17). As a nation, we have forgotten him. Draw the necessary conclusion.

Even so, the worst imaginable judgment has not occurred. The Lord has not removed his word from our midst (Amos 8:11). In thousands of churches each week, the Bible is opened, read, and proclaimed. If this were our only blessing, we should sing and rejoice! Our blessed Savior has by no means removed our candlestick! In tens of thousands of homes scattered through the land, God is worshipped and his word read by fathers who "understand the times" and will not kiss the image of unbelief, statism, self, and perversity. One line of God's precious word is more powerful than every lie Satan has ever told, than all the inanities and perversities that spew from the airwaves. God's word will crush these idols. God is crushing them; Jesus Christ is going to war against them in response to the pleas of his people. Wickedness is most feverish and appears strongest when it begins to burn out. The lies become more brazen, the perversity less apologetic. Like the priests of Baal, when men cut themselves, rant against God and the Bible, and kill his servants, their fury is not evidence of their victory but of their pending defeat. "When the enemy rushes in like a flood, the Spirit of the Lord will lift up a standard against him" (Isa. 59:19).

Take a deep breath. Remember that the wheat and the tares grow together. This metaphor, as well as those of sowing and reaping, leaven, and trees, indicates that God's purposes take time to ripen. Too many apocalyptic movies with tidy endings have created false expectations of kingdom conflict and victory. The Lord will test our faith; we must learn to carry the cross with patience. It is easy in our age of instant communication to make snap judgments: "If they do this, then it will be end of the world." I seriously doubt it. "Be not afraid of sudden fear, nor of the desolation of the wicked when it cometh; for the Lord shall be thy confidence, and shall keep thy foot from being taken" (Prov. 3:25-26). The endless streaming of information, much of which is selected and packaged in order to sell agendas and products, can easily lead us to think that the world is swirling out of control. It is not. Our King sits above the floods and directs them so that all serve his higher purposes.

If a child throws a tantrum, scatters his toys in a fit of rage, and runs around the room screaming and spitting – as many politicians, pundits, warmongers, and economics are doing since their schemes of "life and liberty" without God simply will not work in his world – a wise parent does not join him. Nor does he discipline with commensurate fury, for this would only exasperate the child and convince him that his parent is a bigger fool than he is. The wicked "are like the troubled sea, when it cannot rest, whose waters cast up mire and dirt. There is no peace, saith my God, to the wicked" (Isa. 57:20-21). Do not be surprised or fearful, therefore, when unbelieving men and nations act like, well, unbelievers. Having no peace of conscience, their lives and actions are not going to be peaceable, measured, or wise. A bad tree bears bad fruit. There is a certain madness associated with sin. It goes from bad to worse, deceived and being deceived (2 Tim. 3:13). God is not troubled by this; neither should we be.

You say, "Well, they may be coming for us." That may be. Daniel knew that they were coming to throw him to the lions, but he carried on as usual with his "morning, noon, and evening" prayers, in plain view, confident that his life was in God's hand. This is the patience of the saints. It explains the calmness of the martyrs, the boldness of Christ's disciples, and the quiet of soul that God gives to us when we are faithful. His wings overshadow us; underneath are the everlasting arms. Is it any wonder that one of our Lord's most common directives is "Do not be afraid?" There is nothing to fear from men. The Lord holds the heart of every man in his hand. If we feared God more, we should fear men less: far less, not at all.

Trusting God's wisdom and protection, we pray for the peace of the city in which we live, for rulers and all who are in authority. We should be nonplussed by all the rage of men, for it will either promote God's praise or be restrained by his power and wisdom (Ps. 76:10). We build houses, go about our callings, raise our families, speak God's truth, call upon men to repent, model repentance and righteousness, and suffer joyfully, confident that God is at the helm of this nation. Time and history are on the side of righteousness, for God is the Creator and Lord of each.

Tell those around you "what great things God has done for you soul." Encourage godly men to stand for righteousness, and ask God to make you such a man or woman in your sphere of influence. Expect for Jesus Christ to drive his enemies mad with rage against his reign and to build his Church in the midst of their fury. He will expose their delusions, and as we are caught up in his march, we shall feel the pinch. Give God no rest until he makes his Church a praise in the earth (Isa. 62:7). He has promised. His enemies are accomplishing his purposes, not theirs. Do not be afraid. "Now is your salvation nearer than when you first believed." The King of the nations is on the march. He will not fail or be disappointed. The pleasure of the Lord will prosper in his hand.

First Things

Everyone wants answers, solutions to the myriads of political, economic, domestic, and foreign conundrums that each day sap a little more of our lingering national life. My guess is that whoever shouts "I can change things" the loudest and with the whitest smile will gain political power for the foreseeable future. The masses feel more than they think, and this virtually assures that the candidate who says the least the most attractively will win. Christians, of course, acutely feel the tumult. We shall hear the regular rounds of argument for the "lesser of two evils," a few isolated voices calling for a new Christian party, and mostly just a great deal of doom and gloom complaining. Others will understandably rub their hands in sarcastic glee. "Now, the other side will learn that they should have listened to us."

To us? What do we honestly have to say about the present situation? Does integrity characterize the majority of Christian men? Can we honestly say that mainstream Christian leaders consistently live by the principles they would ram down the throats of Americans through the ballot box? Taking a broader view, can we deny that our present condition is anything other than deserved? If the way of the transgressor is hard, who are we to complain about hard times when we practice the same fiscal irresponsibility as our national government, albeit on a slightly smaller scale, give over our children to the secularists to be educated, and are guilty of a host of personal sins for which our heavenly Father is chastening us? A free nation, economic prosperity, and peace are not birthrights; they are gifts of God's grace, the fruits of covenant faithfulness that no constitution, centralized government, and charismatic leaders can give or guarantee.

This does not mean, however, that the situation is hopeless. This would be a legitimate conclusion only if we had already determined that the problems of our nation can be repaired by government, whether more or less. Different statism, conservative statism, is not the solution to liberal statism. Marxism by any other name is still Marxism, whether the poster child is Joseph Stalin,

Desmond Tutu, Che Guevara, or the big government candidate du jour. The two national parties are like a ping-pong ball traveling between the same teams; the only difference is the spin each player puts on the ball and the speed of the return.

Those who see the Lamb of God sitting at the right hand of the Father take a different view, and one that creates neither paralyzing pessimism nor despairing indifference. Whoever wins this or the next ten elections, the resurrected Son of God, Jesus Christ, is reigning at the right hand of God. He is the King of this nation, whether we are governed by secularists, pseudo-Christians, Muslims, or Corporate America. As Stephen did, we must see heaven open by faith, and the Son of Man in his glory, interceding and governing over all, standing at the finish line of faith, beckoning us to be faithful in his strength. As we believe that he is the King, that he is carrying out his purposes, and that his appointed weapons have lost not one whit of their power, we shall be greatly encouraged and strengthened.

To this must be added personal, familial, and congregational submission to that King. Are our lives, words, and priorities, not to mention a hundred daily decisions, substantially different from those of the world? Are we a peculiar people, peculiar not because we dress and talk weirdly or are unable to interact meaningfully with those around us, but because we are peculiarly devoted to the enthroned Christ and his word? If even a tithe of the professing Christians in this nation were reformed by God's Spirit to live in such a fashion, we would not need to speculate about the future, for that would speedily reveal itself.

The lost would be converted. The globe would pulsate with kingdom prayers that are focused upon the glory of God and of his enthroned Christ. The practical holiness of believers would present a shocking contrast to the world. Men would listen to our words because they would be winsomely verified by our lives. Kings and Presidents would become nursing fathers to the Church and bow in submission to the King of kings. It is wasteful to get worked up into a lather about the next election. If you want to give serious mental and emotional energy to something, give it to your lost neighbor next door, to supporting your pastor through prayer, and to the holiness of your family.

This is not to abandon the dominion mandate; it is to redirect it where it belongs: to the first things, as Paul calls them, of which the resurrection of the Son of God is the centerpiece (1 Cor. 15:3). It is the first thing because through the resurrection, Jesus Christ was declared to be the Son of God in power, victorious over sin, Satan, and death. It is the first thing because it was immediately followed by his entering into his glory and kingdom, the inheritance promised by his Father as a reward for his obedience, suffering, and death. It is the first thing because it is the proclamation that causes men and nations to tremble (Acts 2:30-37).

Because Christ Jesus our Lord is raised from the dead, the war against sin and Satan has already been won. Christus Victor is our cry. This is his battle, not ours. He has equipped us with divinely empowered weapons that demolish strongholds. When the Church uses these, she is fighting in the power of the first things. We pray and preach; Jesus smites the earth with the rod of his mouth. We witness and love; Jesus causes all men to know that we are his disciples. We repent and seek the grace of Christ; the power of his resurrection enables us to walk in newness of life. We are simple concerning evil and wise concerning good, and Jesus our Savior crushes Satan beneath our feet. This is the way we fight the battle; the first things must influence every other thing.

Our religious legacy in the United States is that we must do something, that true religion is publicly lived-out religion, socially relevant religion. However much we may differ on the nature of God's kingdom, it is remarkable that most Christians are still committed to the idea that we must "build the kingdom of Christ," and that a significant part of that kingdom building is political involvement and social action. At one level, Christ's kingdom and glory in the world must dominate us! But they must be built upon the first things (1 Cor. 15:3). Christian nations, godly leaders, and civil liberty are the fruits of the first things, not the first things themselves. We will never enjoy them if we make them our primary goal; they are secondary blessings, the fruits of multigenerational confession, proclamation, and living the first things. And these first things are far more important and lasting in their relevance and power than the secondary things upon which we seem to have set our hope.

Should you be concerned about the condition of our nation, the quality of its leadership, and the consequences of its sins? Absolutely. Should you seek to do something? Definitely. What? Commune with the enthroned Lamb, live by the word of the enthroned Lamb, and proclaim to everyone the peace terms of the Lamb. Do these first things, and the Father will come to our defense, for he always comes to the defense of his resurrected Son – "the zeal of the Lord of hosts will perform it" (Isa. 9:7). Pray for the Lord Jesus Christ to be glorified, to bless his word, and to confound his enemies. Do these, and you may be sure that your prayers will be sanctified by the intercession of our ever-praying Savior and hurled back upon the earth in the form of judgments upon God's enemies and deliverances for his people.

If we push the first things to the background, or think political action is the only thing that will save America, we will continue to reap the bitter consequences of misdirected dominion. The enthroned Lamb is fighting. He is praying prayers that cannot be frustrated. He is fighting his great war on a million fronts. The sword of the gospel is going out of his mouth. His purposes are not in the least stymied by our present and potential leadership. He is carrying forward his great battle in and through them. The nations will kiss the Son – or be judged. Every knee will bow to him. Are you proclaiming his peace terms: faith and repentance? Are you speaking of his resurrection, the first thing and our only foundation for hope? Are you living in the power of his resurrection, in fellowship with his sufferings, being made conformable to his death?

Through these first things alone, his resurrection life will be operable in your life. Through these first things alone, the nations will be discipled, secularism defeated, and liberty and justice prevail. I firmly believe that the most politically meaningful action believers can take at present is to live and proclaim, with humility joined with courage: Jesus is Lord. This is the one political platform the world hates but which it cannot resist. It is the first thing the apostles declared, the confession of the earliest believers, and the divine power that converts the world: Christ, not man, is King.

~4~
Christ in Us:
In Union with the
Lord of Glory

The Wonder of Jesus

Our Lord often did and said the unexpected. He went through Samaria to seek out one woman; the disciples marveled that he talked with her (John 4:27). On a hillside in Galilee, he told his disciples to feed a multitude with a couple of fish and a loaf of bread. The day after, when this multitude knowingly rejected him as the bread of life, he did not try to make the truth easier for them to accept but twice said: "No man can come unto me unless the Father who sent me draw him" (John 6:44,65). Nor in the secrecy of night would he directly answer Nicodemus' query but pressed him with the necessity of the new birth (John 3:1-12). He asked surprising questions. To his disciples: "Who do you say that I am?" To blind Bartimaeus: "What do you want me to do for you" (Mark 10:48)?

His most famous sermon is filled with beautiful yet surprising words. You are blessed when men persecute you for my sake, so rejoice (Matt. 5:11-12). Security lies not in mountains of money but in asking your Father for daily bread (6:11). Do not worry about clothing, but consider that God clothes the birds and the flowers; he will do the same for you if you seek first his kingdom (6:17-34). The world says to know who your enemies are and to treat them accordingly; Jesus says to love and forgive them. Be like God, who does good to his enemies (5:44).

After three years of unexpected words and works, Jesus continued to astound his disciples. On his last night with them before the cross, he washed their feet and distributed the Passover bread and wine, transformed its significance, and called it his body and blood. He willingly gave himself into the hands of his captors, even directing a very dangerous moment so that the sword did not lose one of his disciples or an enemy's ear.

We do not reckon adequately with something very simple about Jesus Christ our Lord. He is the unexpected; he is marvelous. While he was expected according to the law and the prophets, so that later, the disciples "remembered that these things were written of him and that they had done these things unto him" (John 12:16), this did not diminish their sense of wonder but heightened it. He did not simply fulfill the Scriptures, as if he quoted a verse after everything he did or said. His every word and work was a living, divine unfolding of the Word. He was not what men expected, even when they knew the Scriptures and watched him fulfill thousand year-old prophecies.

Jesus remains this wonderful, astounding, unexpected Savior. Now that he is Lord of all (Rom. 14:9), we should not for one moment think that we can finally settle into a normal life. Life with him is not normal, at least by our fallen expectations. It is pointless to try to normalize Jesus, to tame him, to make him conform to our preferences and comfortable expectations.

We do this even though we truly love him. We find a promise he has made about our children. "Train up a child in the way that he should go, and when he is old, he will not depart from it" (Prov. 22:6). We become like Job's three friends, thinking that he will work in a straight-line, no testing of patience, no crying for grace unto faithfulness and seeking from him the fulfillment of his promise. Since he does not work according to our expectations, we grow frustrated and think some new set of spiritual principles is necessary. No, we need to recover a sense of wonder at him. Most of the time, we see no better than his disciples did that his word is being fulfilled before our eyes. He works in such a way that we are led to trust not that "we did it the right way" but that he is the "Wonderful Counselor, the Mighty God." He will have us feel as his foes did: "No man ever spoke this way." To this we might add, "No man ever worked this way, fulfilled his promises in this way, left us utterly amazed in this way."

It is true that we have his word and promises and that he always acts in accordance with them. Yet, in fulfilling them, he is not bound to act according to our expectations. He will pierce our hearts and expose our idols, fears, and selfishness. He will teach us that we are the ones who need to be tamed, not him. We do not like to be challenged, to have our understanding of his word challenged, even to be challenged by him. We like for things to fit into their appropriate boxes. It is much easier, we think, if everything is where it should be, under our control, going as we planned. To be a disciple of Jesus Christ means that we must give up this silly presumption. If we insist upon being in control, we have lost the wonder of being a disciple of the living Savior and Lord. We have lost the essence of what it means to serve our Master. He, not we, directs all things and knows the master plan.

Losing wonder, we lose our sense of needing to draw near to him. Peter sees Jesus walking on the water, and nothing will do but that he must go to Jesus on the stormy sea. The bleeding woman hears a dreaded question: "Who touched me" (Luke 8:25)? She cannot slink away but must come to Jesus and tell him everything, in front of everyone. The Samaritan woman is completely exposed by Jesus, but she must go tell all the men in her city about a man who "told me all things that ever I did" (John 4:29). Paul and Silas are bleeding for preaching the gospel, but they must sing praise to him.

Jesus Christ is wonderful. The heart feels safe, the soul whole, only in closeness to him. The thoughts are scattered and confused until he comes through his word and Spirit and teaches us wisdom. Our tears need his hand, his comfort, his "My peace I give to you" (John 14:27). If Jesus Christ were other than he is, the living, reigning Lord of wonder, we would not feel this need. Since he is all these things beyond our capacity to imagine, we are drawn to him. We must have him.

Much is said today about a "personal" relationship with Jesus Christ. The phrase is abused and overused, but its core truth is vital. Jesus Christ our Lord is a person. He is real; he is reality. He is the eternal Word who made all things. He is the incarnate Word who has saved all things. He is the abiding Word who continues to make his presence known in those convicting moments when like a lightning flash he shows us, as he did Peter, what is really in our hearts and that he alone can heal us. He is known in suffering times, when we feel strangely strengthened to press forward, trusting, crawling toward him.

When we come to him, he will transform us. "Behold, I make all things new" (Rev. 21:5). The transformation process in his disciples never stops. We never reach a place where he is boxed; where life is boxed and tidy, or even boxed and hopeless. We never reach a place where we should say, "Well, this is just the way I am – or my wife is, or my children are." Fellowship with Jesus Christ is personally, powerfully, incredibly transforming. Being a Christian is wonderful, for Jesus Christ is wonderful. It is also personally sifting and often painful.

Remember, however, that we are his disciples, followers of him wherever he leads. Discipleship is consecration to him out of love for his person and work and words. Becoming part of a movement, gaining personal notoriety, standing for social causes, or aligning oneself with men are unworthy, impotent, and ultimately dissatisfying reasons for discipleship. He rejected (John 2:23-25) all other reasons for discipleship except one: "If you love me." "If anyone will come after me." "Deny yourself, take up your cross, and follow me" (John 14:15; Luke 9:23). Disciples of Jesus love Jesus, study him, imitate him, learn of him, draw near to the Father through him, believe in his blood, trust his righteousness, and gladly obey his commands. This the essence of the Christian discipline: "That I may know him" (Phil. 3:10). "For me, to live is Christ" (Phil. 1:21).

To be his disciples, therefore, means that we dictate no terms of service to him. We reserve no area of our lives where he is forbidden to go, prohibited to expose with his wisdom, convict with his word, or humble by his majesty. Neither a holy life nor the soundest theology is a fence to protect us from his searching and sifting of our hearts. To know him, we must pray daily:

"Lord, where we need to be chastened, chasten. Where we need to be humbled, humble. Where our children need more tenderness or discipline or understanding, give us from your fullness of grace what we completely lack in ourselves. Teach us that you are our only good and that we can take no credit for anything. Teach us that fellowship with you is our life and happiness. Lord, we are yours; we want to live for you, to be led and governed by you; we want to be tamed; we want to know you. Give us your life-giving Spirit of wisdom. Abide with us through your word. Make what we learn effectual to enflame our hearts with awe before your majesty and humility before your sufferings.

Make it true of us as it was of the apostle: 'For me, to live is Christ.'"

Get in the word, disciple, and there stand in awe of Jesus Christ. When he is wonderful to you, being a Christian will fill you with wonder. Obedience, peace, joy, passion, and usefulness will follow. Our wonderful Savior will give them.

Hidden Life

Our Lord gives many gospel glories: forgiveness of sins, peace with God, the indwelling Spirit with his gifts and graces, and a completed revelation. Yet the full glory of our salvation is hidden. The glories that lie ahead for the child of God are known dimly when revealed at all. And we often forget that our earthly lives are of infinitesimal duration and experience in comparison to everlasting life, to what shall be. Absorption with the present life is thus unwise and ultimately frustrating. Yes, we are to serve the Lord in our generation, but the eye of faith simultaneously focuses upon the future, upon what lies ahead.

This dual perspective is a necessary discipleship dynamic. We are to revel in the glorious realities we now possess in Christ while longing for the greater glories that lie ahead. Consider Colossians 3:1-4. Paul begins by stating that if or since we have been raised with Christ, we are to seek the things that lie above, where Christ reigns at the right hand of the Father. Through the regenerating work of the Holy Spirit, we experience the death of sin through the death of Christ. Through his resurrection, we are raised to new life. And since we have died and have been raised with Christ, we are to seek the things above: the power of Christ's reign in our lives, communion with him through prayer and saturation with his word, and our future destiny with him when the full redemption of the sons of God will be understood and experienced in ways we cannot presently fathom. This is what we are to seek: an earthly life of faithfulness, usefulness, and discipleship empowered through the reign of our Savior, animated by desire to be with him, encouraged by intense reflection upon our future with him.

And our affections – how misspent they often are! Our minds or affections must be "set on the things above." The verb means to reflect upon intently, to have a high regard for, to respect. The "things above" refers specifically to the glorious person and mediatorial work of Jesus Christ. We are to think often and deeply upon these things. This refers first and foremost to the position of Jesus Christ and our position in him. It is only as we look at him that we understand a portion of what we shall be. It is only as we abide in him that we are able to experience the first-fruits of future glory in our earthly lives.

To set one's affections on things above, then, indicates that the glories of heaven must occupy the first place in our hearts – not this life, not our problems, not even sin. Christ – his victory – our victory in him – our future with him: toward these glories all our affections must strain. Our best thoughts must focus there. Our most fervent desires must strive to be there – with Jesus Christ, where he is. Whatever is done on earth can only be done well as our affections are firmly fixed upon the eternal, the incorruptible, and the lasting.

We are not to set our affections on things below. This is indeed a great challenge. Billions of men live and die having spent their entire existence absorbed with this life – money, security, health. And even with respect to the many good things below that occupy our time and energies – family, piety, work, and extension of gospel influence – it is possible to be immersed in them with the wrong perspective – too focused upon the here and now. We labor here, and we labor diligently in hope. Our citizenship, however, is in heaven, and whatever progress the kingdom of Jesus Christ enjoys on earth, it will always come far behind the glories that await us.

If we set our affections on things below, we will always be disappointed. Imagine how the Puritans would feel if they saw what has become of their "city set on a hill." Granted, it is man's faithlessness that has given up the noble aspects of their vision and misspent their spiritual capital. Yet at the same time, we can only regain what good has been lost and improve upon it if our affections lie in heaven. Affections set upon the glory of God and the honor of Jesus Christ motivate and empower us to kingdom prayer, serious evangelistic efforts, sacrifice of money and time, and self-denial – all with joy, because all in Christ, directed to him, guided by his word, loving him, trusting his promised presence through the Holy Spirit.

The reason we cannot set our affections on things below, Paul adds in verse 3, is because we are dead, and our lives are hidden with Christ in God. It is odd to think oneself dead, but in Christ we are – dead to the dominion of sin, dead to the offerings of an unbelieving world, dead to our old desires and priorities. Union with Jesus Christ brings a decisive end to the tyranny of sin, Satan, and death. Our new lives are hidden with Christ. This is profound. Our lives are bound to his – his victory, his reign, his glorious entrance into heaven, his preparing a place for us. This is our life. Christ is our life. We cannot lead a God-honoring and satisfying life below, therefore, unless it is the Christ-life.

This is more than a life of warm feelings and mystical heavenly mindedness. It is certainly not a life of general morality, universal tolerance, and a simple "love your neighbor" without biblical definitions of love. It is the life of death to sin and self through ongoing fellowship with Christ empowering us to holiness. It is the life of zeal for the Father's glory that directs us to hate sin, labor for the glory and honor of God to fill the earth. It is the life of consecrated obedience to the will of God revealed in Scripture, for this was the life of our Savior and the only way to happiness and peace (John 14:15,21; 15:9-11). Unless we strive by the power of the Spirit to be obedient to the totality of God's word as he was, we cannot have his life within us. But this life is still hidden. We have this treasure in jars of clay. We understand some rudiments of it and experience some of its power. We also struggle and cry. We are sometimes defeated by sin. Death is still painful. But we remember that our lives are hidden with Christ.

And as we live this way, death becomes less terrifying to us. O, it is awful, awful, but it is not unbearable or hopeless. Our Savior's resurrection guarantees that we will have life after death, spiritually and one day physically. The reason Paul can say that to depart and be with Christ is far better than this earthly existence is that our lives are perfected only in him. Paul longed to depart and be with Christ. Yes, he longed to die. He longed to die that he might fully live in Christ. His death wish did not produce melancholy, earthly irrelevance, or stoicism. It energized. He understood that as long as it pleased Christ for him to live, his life on earth would be an unfolding of Christ's power through his weakness. Thus, believer, do not fear death. Welcome it when it comes. Welcome it as the perfection of your life in Christ. Welcome it as the beginning of the unhidden life of Christ in you.

When you see the glory of Christ sitting at the right hand of the Father, you will be transformed. Do not hold on to this life as if it were the consummation of all that is good and enjoyable. Live in Christ and labor in Christ. No one who understands that our lives are hidden with Christ in God is lazy, indifferent to the evil of his times, or backward in defending the interests of Jesus Christ and the life and immorality that has now appeared in history through his gospel. But do these things with the eye of faith fixed upon the finish line of faith.

Additional incentive to a mind fixed upon things above is contained in verse 4. Christ shall appear, and then the glory of our life in him will be fully manifested, for we shall appear with him. We will reign with him, be perfected in him, judge with him, and be crowned with him. It is true that we do not see these things now, but we do see Jesus (Heb. 2:9). We see what he now enjoys, and we labor in faith that these glories will one day be ours. Our future life is known now only in him, as we behold him where he is by faith, walk with him in obedience, and set our affections on him.

This is the faith that sustained Abraham, David, the prophets, and the apostles. The same faith will sustain us, if we will use this life without abusing it, do not allow our faith and hope to rise and fall with the fortunes of the city of man, and shun the evil dreams and distractions of the secularists. Faithless men never see anything beyond this life, and they never see it correctly because they do not see it in the light of Jesus Christ and his reign at the right hand of the Father. Do not listen to them, adopt their priorities, have their worries. You have Christ. His life will progressively unfold in you as you walk with him.

Joy Is a Person

Joy is elusive, the path easily missed, the feeling mistaken for the substance, the rays for the sun. Look in the wrong place, and your life will be frustration. Some look for joy in literature and philosophy, the thoughts of fellow-pilgrims about joy. You will only go as far as they have gone, err where they have erred. Ascend with them to the heights of logic and beauty; follow their insights into the so-called human condition and the way to overcome it. The lightning may flash, shining for a moment on the wasteland of human folly, illumining, you think, joy. The descent to earth must come: a return to longing.

Others seek joy in nature; many poets have taken us there. Nature only shows that joy and beauty exist; it cannot give them. Nature itself is waiting for joy. Science does not give joy; it only attempts an explanation for processes. Sometimes it divinizes them, and thinks it has found all the joy there is in cataloguing, experimenting, at its worst, controlling and manipulating. This is not joy but sorcery; playing at God is pretending to have joy.

All earth-bound joy – nature, possessions, science, pleasure – are debunked as sources of joy by one consideration: man himself. Man must be put into each of these scenarios, and when he is, they are shown to be vapid, even destructive. He may in the spring of his life find resemblance to himself in beautiful flowers, green trees, and rushing rivers; winter is coming. He may be blessed with abundance, but death is coming. It is folly to tightly clutch to what always flies away. Make science as the way to joy through man's control of his environment, and the sterility of the test tube and scrutiny of the microscope dehumanize him. Make him a cog in the wheel of a political system or economic program, and he stops smiling. Drudgery engulfs him.

At some point, searching the plateaus and valleys of human experience for joy will prove dissatisfying. Each man must return home. Perhaps joy is to be found in a quiet life of family and calling. But joy is not the same thing as the pleasure we take in our spouse and children, a good day's work, a carefully tended garden. The thorn pricks your finger, your boss cannot be pleased, and your children exasperate: the feeling of pleasure soon flees. The same problems are found in friendship, and at a lower level in hobbies, games, and gadgets. Momentary pleasure, even personal fulfillment, diminishes over time. The search continues.

We turn to God for joy, something solid, lasting, above and outside us. There are many versions of this path. Plato tried "the soul takes flight to the world that is invisible," but the soul only finds escape there and loses itself altogether. The God of Plato is essentially the eternal source of the same soul that is seeking escape. We cannot know him, relate to him, or be joyful in him. Later, God became the "unmoved Mover," the concrete Absolute. He is something beyond us, giving stability in a world of change. He must exist, or all our experience here is rubbish. God may be necessary on this scheme, but he is personally unknowable. No joy to be found here – perhaps pure logic, pure mind, a cosmic guarantor, but very dissatisfying. Cold, tidy systems make relieved, self-assured, momentarily satisfied partisans. They do not give joy.

We turn to the God of the Bible. At least he purports to speak, to be knowable, personal, near to us in Jesus. But in our present confusion, we find that there are as many interpretations of this God as there are men who claim to know him. Then, these very God-promoters are often bickering. There is sadness in the thought that the proliferation of churches and systems of theology often point to past religious wars. This is not at all to disparage the richness of God's word or the importance of holding to all he has said, joy in all its brilliant facets. Yet, when secondary and tertiary points of doctrine and practice become the dividing line of friend from foe, orthodox from heretic, joy departs. We have left the first things, as Paul describes them (1 Cor. 15:3), confusing the root of joy for its fruits.

When first things, which alone give first love and first joy, lose their hold upon our souls, it is not surprising that we demand others to take our view on everything else: anything to keep the diminishing joy and find its fullness again. That we are now disinterested and dismissive of these religious wars, even laugh at those poor fools who died for what we think obscure principles, does not mean we have matured. It only points to the lack of seriousness with which we take the words of God. Better to stand and fight for clarity of joy than pursue it as we now do: as a private affair of the heart, huddled up with those who blandly profess to think the same as we do in order to avoid conflict. By this we miss the joy God spreads throughout his vineyard. One container is too small for its enormity, for him.

Joy is found in the God of the Bible, but we must be careful. Joy is not God abstractly considered, philosophically contemplated, God interpreted through the lens of our personal experience. It is not God without church. It is certainly not the God of the free-spirited seeker, who wants joy on his terms without the pinch of being told, even by God, what he must believe, how he must worship, and the way he must live. If joy is to be found in God, it must be on his terms, not ours. He is very self-centered. With him alone is self-centeredness a holy attribute. Jealous is a better and more biblical word. He is jealous for himself, for he is joy, as the psalmist says. He is also jealous for us. He carefully, purposefully fashioned us to possess only one joy, the only joy there is.

If to this we add sin – and all sin is ultimately the pursuit of joy in false ways that lead us away from God, from truth and righteousness – we confront an impassable barrier to joy. We cannot get to God. Spend all your life consulting the philosophers and trying to resolve sin's intellectual and moral mess, and you will get no closer to God. The lives of the philosophers are often the best refutation of their systems. The last two centuries of machines, control, convenience, and economic planning have brought more blood, more dissatisfaction, more delusion, and less joy. I wonder if the washerwoman living in a house with a dirt floor was not far happier than the cleanest urbanite with all her gadgets. Compare the old hymns and even folk music with what passes today for popular music. A modern man may have a thousand friends through technology but not one true Jonathan. We have harnessed steam, fire, atoms, and conductive metals; we have pushed joy far away, confusing it with instant directional help, access to exotic foods from around the world, and everything standardized, mechanized, processed. This is not the fault of technology. We took the wrong path with it, demanded more than it could give. We thought it would lead us to God without having to make the pilgrim's progress, without having to face our true need.

Thus, we are confronted with a single door through the barrier: Jesus Christ. He is joy because he is God; he is joy because he is man. As God, he speaks to us with full authority and majesty, light in our darkness, joy in our misery. As man, he draws near to us, entering fully into the sorrow and grief of our fallen condition, bearing our curse upon his beaten back. Can we ever exhaust the mystery of joy recovered through blood atonement? John 3:16 is not a slogan for simpletons; it is the most profound invitation to joy: sinners loved by God in Christ; sinners saved from death by his death on the cross, sinners redeemed unto obedience so that they might walk in harmony with God. To have this joy, we must have Jesus Christ, for he is the one gate who ushers us back into the presence of joy, into the comfortable presence of God.

Anything else or less is to accept ultimate misery, inexplicable mystery: no answers to life's problems, no directions for the safe use of technology, no limits on human tyranny, systems without substance, experience without infallible interpretation, man alone. Reject him and reject joy. Embrace him, and find joy everywhere, dispersed in all his many gifts, diamonds of heaven scattered throughout the universe. He is not a narrow joy, to have only on Sundays or while reading the Bible. He is joy in work, art, philosophy, and technology, for he recovers their true purpose and guides them along a sure path. Rightly used, they all lead back to him, for he is the joyful source of all wisdom and knowledge.

He is also joy in human relations, for through friends and family, even those who differ from us on secondary points, he draws us to himself, shows another spark of his fullness. He is joy even in this vale of sin, for he illumines and gives the beauty of grace, forgiveness, and hope. He is joy everywhere for he is Lord of all. He is joy everywhere for he is "God with us." He is eternal joy. When the curtain of this life drops, it will rise to the sight of his loving gaze, his exalted splendor, his unending, satisfying presence, his "Well done" giving joy unspeakable and full of glory, life with him, in him, and unto him forever.

Being with Jesus

When Peter and John stood before the Sanhedrin, something unexpected occurred. Two months earlier, the Jewish leaders had done away with Jesus. Silencing his disciples should be quick work: warnings, beatings, perhaps some jail time, a death or two. With the striking of the shepherd, the sheep would be easily scattered. The Sanhedrin was completely unprepared for the personal effect Jesus had upon Peter and John.

Before them stood two unlearned and ignorant men, of no account, despised commoners. Suddenly, Peter and John reversed the examination; sheer boldness and clear proclamation turned the accused into the accusers, the condemned into judges. Instead of denying their Lord or being overcome with fear, Peter and John steadfastly professed the name of Jesus Christ, directly pointed the sword of the Spirit at our Savior's murderers, and preached salvation in no other name but Jesus. Defeated by the Son of God in his death, the Sanhedrin is now defeated by his living power in his lowly disciples. They cannot deny the notable healing, but they must not allow this name to be preached, this doctrine to spread. Their own criminality would surely become known; their tyrannical stranglehold over the people would be threatened.

After a few minutes of private council, the Sanhedrin could do nothing but forbid them to preach in Jesus' name. Insufficient ground even for a beating was present. Peter and John, however, refused to be dismissed so easily. Hearing the Sanhedrin's threat, they calmly said: "No. We will obey God rather than you. We have a clear duty; we shall not abandon our posts. We cannot but speak the things we have seen and heard." Being with Jesus changed everything for Peter and John.

It has been said that the secret of Christian influence depends upon being much in the company of Jesus. True, we have not known his physical presence, though we greatly long for it. To depart and be with him is better by far than anything else on earth. Until then, however, he is with us by his Spirit, a covenanted presence of grace and power, life and joy, anointing and light. That we are often so lifeless, dull, and impotent is to be attributed more than anything else to our failure to avail ourselves of his fellowship. We are not often with Jesus.

That our words, even our Christian words to our family and friends, often seem perfunctory and preachy, exhibiting more party-spirit than sincere love and personal commitment to our Savior, may be traced to the same cause. We are not adoringly with Jesus. That we focus upon the symptoms of our fellow-sinners' diseases rather than lovingly pointing them to the Great Physician, is also the result of too little fellowship with our Savior, too little experience of the joy and grace of his presence in our lives. If we are with Jesus, he does great things for us. These great things we warmly share with such earnestness, simplicity, and humility that men, like the Sanhedrin, cannot but note that we have been with Jesus.

Our Savior invites us to his fellowship by calling us to "abide in him." This is prefaced by his declaration of an objective engrafting into him that each of us experiences when we are born again. We are definitively and covenantally united with him by the inward renewing and sealing work of the Holy Spirit. At the same time, we are to "abide in him." We are to live in his company. His word is to be our constant companion, for his word is spirit and life, absolutely and effectually. We are to draw from him – through believing prayer, faith in his promises, and dependence upon his grace – all life, light, glory, and blessedness.

To abide in Christ, we must walk by the Spirit (Gal. 5:16). We do this by mortifying sin through repentance, confession, self-denial, and seeking our life in him. We walk by the Spirit as we put on the new man through renewing the mind in the truth and obeying God's commands. Life in the Spirit is life in the word of Jesus. The Spirit of holiness and truth is the living bond and abiding presence of Jesus with us. As we walk by the Spirit, we shall bear much fruit, drawing from Jesus his fruit and fullness, grace upon grace (Phil. 1:11; John 1:16).

Being with Jesus is not mysticism. It is not a higher life of following an inner light, which is really nothing more than following our own impulses. It is not the result of occasional

122

thoughts about God, content when a few snippets of the Bible flit about in our heads with no exercising of the will, emotion, and mind toward the Son of God and his word. We will never be with Jesus by following spiritual gurus or participating in a score of new and creative church programs, which are so ubiquitous in our age exactly because we are not more with Jesus himself. He makes spiritual gimmicks and worship circuses unnecessary for the maturing believer. No, nothing substitutes for being with Jesus: with him in his word, with him in prayer, with him in his worship and sacraments, with him in meaningful service and fellowship with other believers. With him we must be, for an "out there" Savior, a theoretical Savior, a merely intellectually apprehended and historically embraced Savior, will never save or satisfy a single soul. We must have Jesus Christ himself, in all his divine glory, immeasurable love, and transforming grace. We must be with him.

There are impediments to being with him. We encounter several of these in the gospel. Some would not follow him fully because they would not forsake their family (Luke 9:59-61). A modern application of this would be allowing family demands, schedules, and sins to prevent true and constant fellowship with Christ and his body. Others were afraid of losing pecuniary advantage and the comforts of the world (Luke 9:57-58). One thinks here of those who are not with Jesus in their business practices, or for whom covetous thoughts choke out the delight of knowing and being with Jesus. Still others lost the incomparable blessing of being with Jesus because they were too much in love with this world; their interests were divided (Luke 9:62). It is certain that we will never yield ourselves fully to the joy of being with Jesus as long as either the pleasures or cares of the world so weigh us down that we never establish our complete happiness in him.

By far, however, the real dividing line is the actual claims Jesus made. When he said that we must "eat his flesh" and "drink his blood," many of his early disciples turned away from him (John 6:66). Jesus proclaimed himself as the fulfillment of the peace offering, of which the worshipper partook as a sign and seal of restored fellowship with God. Many would prefer the Jesus of feeling rather than the Jesus of concrete revelation. They would have Jesus feed their bodies, clothe them, and prosper their businesses, but they would not be fed in their souls, for this would require a troublesome renovation of the entire life. It would be to admit that we are completely empty without him. Being with Jesus, though, does exactly this. It is unavoidable. It is often painful, for nothing is more uncomfortable than for us to face ourselves honestly and deeply. Unless we do, we shall never run to Jesus as the only cure of our contagion.

Nothing surpasses being with Jesus. To know his love, his presence, and his power, is to be filled with the fullness of God (Eph. 3:19). Being with him gives compelling reality to our words and witness. He gives us his boldness, as he did to Peter and John. He fills us with a growing sight of his glory. He satisfies our soul. He leads us to seek the Father and say, "Not my will, but thine be done." He consumes us with his zeal for his Father's house. He makes us humble, meek, transparent, and heavenly minded. He breaks the grip of worldliness, lust, and anger. He makes us loving, self-forgetting, self-denying. He invigorates us to love his word, his church, his elders, his worship, his service. He does so much more – more than we can ask or imagine. Being with Jesus is our life.

Lord Over Despair

The old hymn asks: "Art thou weary? Art thou languid?" Many of us are. Some suffer from diseases that are not necessarily fatal or even debilitating but that nonetheless nag, weaken, and distract. Others suffer quietly from miserable relationships, broken hearts, or lost children. The death of a close family member or friend often leaves a wound that never entirely heals. A particular sin is your constant tormentor.

You seek a cure, with greater or lesser intensity, but it lingers, haunts, paralyzes. Sometimes you think victory is won, but in a moment of weakness, the old enemy topples your pillar of confidence and returns you to the valley of despair. You may be waiting for your marriage to heal, for your children to stop breaking your heart, for a better vocation, for financial stability, or for a suitable marriage partner, someone to love. Each one of us, no matter what our outward circumstances, suffers from a lifelong battle with indwelling sin, a contagion that is slowing sapping our energy and vitality, literally killing us as we rot away from the inside. So, yes, we must honestly affirm, "I am weary."

As Jesus was walking in Jerusalem, he came to the pool at the sheep market near Bethesda (John 5:1-17). At this pool lay a great multitude of sick and despairing folk. Their personal stories would melt the hardest heart: blind men, lame women, sick children – in an age without support groups and social nets beyond the family, among men who usually equated personal tragedy with personal wickedness, thus compounding the loneliness and intensifying the despair. These miserables gathered at this pool to seek healing.

An angel occasionally touched the water. Thereafter, the first one to step into the pool was healed. That God occasionally visited his people in such ways should not surprise us. In that long epoch of waiting for the Messiah, he gave testimonies to the daughter of Zion that he had not forgotten her cries or abandoned her to despair. At this pool lay a lame man, a man who had been unable to walk for thirty-eight years: thirty-eight years of waiting, of misery, of watching life go by, of expectation and dashed hopes. How could he hope to reach the pool before others? He could not

125

walk. But he continued to come, hoping for a personal miracle before the main one – that he would get to the pool first.

Jesus came to the pool. In those three years, Jesus sought out, received, and healed many tens of thousands of despairing, broken souls. Jesus saw the man lying by the pool. O, if this man had known what this gaze would soon mean for him, his soul would have been elevated to heaven even as he lay helpless on the ground! For Jesus to look upon us with compassion, his pity joined with power, his soul-penetrating look, knowing and feeling our misery in a moment, is life itself. Note that he looked specifically at this man. A multitude lay nearby, but his merciful gaze fell upon this particular man. Why? Sovereign grace and goodness. He knew the man had been in this condition for a long time. He set his love upon him. He spoke to him.

"Do you want to be made whole" (v. 6)? A strange question on the surface, but does not misery often lead a sufferer to forget its cause, a sinner drowning in his circumstances to forget the sin? Face your hopelessness; but look at me! As this was Jesus' first public visit to Jerusalem, the lame man had no way of knowing who addressed him. "I have no one to take me to the water after the angel troubles it," he said. He had often tried to make it on his own. How? Crawling. How else could a lame man move? Imagine the thoughts in his heart when he saw the water move, how he must have scrutinized the water until he could count almost every drop. Each step between him and the water was measured. Healing was a few steps away; he could not make it. He had tried repeatedly. The physical effort must have been as nothing, however, in comparison to the torment of soul as he saw others, who had diseases that did not impair their movement, rushing toward the pool. Despairingly, he must have halted the effort many times. In an instant, Jesus knew all this. Enough. "Rise, take up thy bed, and walk" (v. 9). Immediately, the man was made whole, took up his bed, and walked.

Unlike some of Jesus' more personal encounters, we are not told anything about this man's faith, response, or subsequent efforts to tell everyone about Jesus. There was no opportunity, for Jesus "conveyed himself away." He did not want to be thronged by the multitude. The healed man had no opportunity to learn the name of his benefactor who instantly altered his life. After an encounter with some furious Jews, for Jesus had done this work of mercy on the Sabbath, Jesus found him in the temple. "Sin no more," he told him, "lest a worse thing come upon you" (v. 14). Jesus hereby encouraged him to view his healing as a call to seek the true healing of soul without which physical health is hardly a blessing. The man went and told the Jews that Jesus had healed him, information, I pray, more prompted by righteous zeal than malice.

We cannot be reminded often enough that the compassion of our Savior is our salvation. Whatever our personal miseries may be, however long we may have suffered from them, or how much effort we may have expended in pursuit of a remedy, he looks upon us with compassion. He entered into our world of despair and suffering, all brought on by sin. He bore our weakness and carried our burdens in his holy, tender soul – because he loved us and would deliver us. A great deal of our victory is simply looking to him, knowing that he looks upon us with his special love and concern, is always ready to help us, prays for us, and exerts all of his blood-bought dominion to bring the comforts of grace to our haggard hearts.

Consider Jesus. Think again and again of his compassion upon the nameless thousands and millions who have looked to him for help, when all other helps failed, because there was no other help. Remember that he gave you the faith to look to him in the first place, for he knew you could not, would not bring yourself to him. He came to you. If you know him, it is because he singled you out in love and pity – not because you were worthy but because you were helpless and hopeless. Do not despair. Be of good cheer! The Son of God has looked upon you and, having looked, he never turns his eyes away.

Think, then, of your causes for despair. Have they not paralyzed you time and again, filled you with fear, dampened your zeal, and left you hopeless? You try to forget them. Virtually all of the world's offerings are designed to lure you into forgetfulness – of your true self, of the true source of your despair, of your true and only Savior. Or, you have tried to cure them yourself. God uses means, so we must use them all. Yet, how often have we used these means with a spirit of self-reliance, without casting ourselves upon the compassion and goodwill of our Savior? Means pursued independently of Jesus may succeed, but a cure without Jesus making us whole creates another kind of misery. So, the despair deepens. We try to nail the cross to our own back. We can make it to the pool this time, we think to ourselves. We fail.

Deliverance from the tyranny of despair is found only by turning full-face to Jesus Christ, the lover of our souls, the Lord over despair. He is more powerful than your suffering. You have endured quietly, perhaps to such a degree that you have grown introverted into an existence of self-pitying despair. Repent of this. The Lord Jesus calls you to look to him and run your race with patience. He may not change your circumstances all at once; perhaps he will not change them at all. He will show you that he is Lord over them, intends to bring good from them, and even more, will show you his power in your weakness.

And here we reach the fountain of despair. We do not truly know ourselves. Our suffering, we think in some deep crevice of our selfish hearts, is really undeserved. I have been treated badly. No one understands me. God has not treated me fairly. Pride this is, sheer pride, and God hates it. And pride is the great quicksand of the soul, for it deceives, embitters, and swallows alive.

We always deserve worse than we receive. Yet, let us once look at the holy, majestic God and upon our holy, beautiful Savior, and we shall be done with all excuses, blaming, and self-pity. One thought will dominate: his promise of mercy and grace to help in our time of need. Jesus will make us beautiful despite our sin and weakness. He turns our despair into dancing, perhaps not immediately but surely and finally. Through sorrow, he calls us to return to him. He makes us whole as we rest in him as our hope and joy.

Finding Life

Satan's first lie to man remains his most alluring: "Ye shall be as gods" (Gen. 3:5). Do what you want to do. Reject anyone who says you should not. Demonize God for not letting you be God. The arch-deceiver hid the consequences of believing his lie. The more we serve self and try to manipulate reality, circumstances, and relationships to suit us, the more miserable we become. To make self your god is to create a personal hell.

Though the horrors of men still listening to this lie appear every hour, it is shocking how much hell believers try to carry into heaven. Think not first of the notorious sins, which receive the most attention but are not necessarily the worst. The respectable sins of pride, ego, and ambition have eroded as many souls as crashing ocean waves upon the shore. Craving admiration and acceptance has left many bitter and sullen. Disappointment that others do not think as highly of you and your opinions as you do shrivels and isolates the soul as few things can. We cannot extract these poisons. They draw the very life out of us and make us unable to love others except insofar as it makes us feel good about ourselves or furthers our personal agendas. Sin has made us a living corpse.

Jesus said, "He that findeth his life shall lose it" (Matt. 10:39). Nothing seems more counterintuitive than to find one's life or happiness, only to lose happiness by obtaining what you thought was happiness. Scripture and experience unite in common witness to this truth. The more we strive for what we think will make us happy, the more happiness slips away.

It is as if God has built an insurmountable wall, barring the way to happiness in the direction of self. You try to make others like you; they like you less or only artificially. You try to make your children conform to your expectations, only to have them follow your lead by elevating their expectations to chief place. You feel frustrated and disillusioned with your current church body and think a change will do you good; the greener grass soon browns under your feet, for you have taken you with you. You try to make your husband or wife better, but they seem to grow worse and more distant.

In society, we spend exponentially more on education than a generation or two ago, but there is less good thinking, reading, and writing now than in several centuries. Wherever we turn, we hit this wall. Seek happiness on your terms; lose happiness. Try to manipulate others into accepting your definition of happiness, or godliness, or success, and you lose them and grow bitter yourself. If I could only have this, be this, do this, be recognized as this; fill in your "this." It is your hell pretending to be heaven.

We see this well enough in the lives of the lost, but do we see it in ourselves? What is our heart set upon? Some of us live with constant frustration that we are not getting to do what we really want to do. Are we asking God to govern our lives the way he wants them to go, or do we love him only when he kneels to our demands? Do we accept that he is God, or is Satan's lie still echoing in our hearts? Do we try to serve our Lord with joy and faithfulness where he has placed us? We should not wonder that our circumstances never seem to change or improve if we are not. When we yield to him, the Lord multiplies small talents and opportunities faithfully used into larger ones – or perhaps not larger, just more wisdom to see that the small ones were the really big ones all the time.

We must lose ourselves to find ourselves. We must join in God's great work of smashing the idols of the human heart. You read a book on the "Wonderful Husband." You look at your husband; he does not seem very wonderful. You try to make him wonderful. Classes and counseling do not work. Perhaps you try manipulation and browbeating or silence and sulking. He runs in the opposite direction. Then, you develop a martyr's complex and find some twisted pleasure in victimizing yourself, pitying yourself as a wife-martyr. Husbands can do the same. There is a little of the false martyr in all of us. But this is not loving one's spouse as you find him but demanding that he measure up to your ideal. Even if that ideal is biblical, we lose and find ourselves by giving God his rightful place as the sole sanctifier of men. In whatever weakness we find our spouse, we are to help and encourage him. We must live as God has commanded for Jesus' sake. Were we good before Jesus would love and lay down his life for us? What of Peter? The Lord washed a devil's feet (John 6:70)! God loved us when we were dead in sin.

Life and happiness must come from outside us. They come only from Jesus Christ, who is the life eternally as the Son of God and as our Mediator by having all life in himself for sinners. He tells us the way to this life. "And he who loses his life for my sake shall find it" (Matt. 10:39). One immediately thinks of true martyrs, and they are certainly included. Yet few ever went to the stake calmly without first learning death to self in a thousand ways. There is first that release of one's demands about life to the Lord. Following closely on the heels of this blessed release, there is that finding of joy in the Lord when life goes in every direction but the one you would choose. Death to self also involves deliverance from fear, inordinate self-love, and clinging to this life as the highest good. We might well call this life in Jesus deliverance from the demands of our fallen self. This is the first step of discipleship, of coming after Jesus: "Let him deny himself" (Matt. 16:24). It is also the redemption of self.

The life we find in Jesus Christ is more than a negation. It is certainly not a negation of all things physical, as if life were a release into some sort of Platonic, spiritual paradise. The life Jesus Christ gives to us required his incarnation, his "in-fleshing." Though many have stumbled over this, the incarnation of the Son of God shows us that life is not escape from the world of sense but its heavenly renewal. When we deny ourselves to find life in him, he gives us life everywhere. He turns our work environments and domestic chores into holy service to him. He saves our homes from disorder and chaos, bringing with him his order and peace through righteousness. He brings life into broken and frustrated relationships by delivering us from the demands, selfishness, and expectations of self. By teaching men that all the treasures of wisdom and knowledge are found in him, he saves education and gives life to mathematics, history, and grammar. The gospel of Jesus Christ is not spiritual platitudes disconnected from man's temporal responsibilities. Just as the Son of God became flesh, his gospel brings the eternal to bear upon the temporal – redeeming, sanctifying, and transforming it.

At the heart of a saved world, saved families, and saved economies are found saved men who have found life in Jesus Christ. He says, "He who loses his life for my sake will find it." The "it" is life, the true life he created us to have but that we lost by believing Satan's lie. Have you ever talked to a believer that seems to look at life differently? He seems to be unmoved by the problems and desires that engulf many. This is not because he does not feel pain or is untried by the Lord in all the ways common to men. It is because he has life. He has Jesus Christ. Pain and sorrow lead him back to life. Troubles lead him to call upon his Lord. He is alive. He has found life. Christ Jesus the Life has changed everything for him. He is not dominated by self. He has to fight against the cravings and temptations of the flesh, but he does so from a position of strength and renewal, of true life in Jesus Christ. When he falls into sin, he runs back to the Life. He returns home, trusting that God is his Father, loves him, and freely forgives his sins. And having found that life, he wants to grow in it, to be found in Christ, to be righteous and holy in his Savior, to suffer and be raised with his Lord.

The gospel call that goes out to all men is to forsake the misery of self and to find life in Jesus Christ. If we have heard his voice and been raised to new life, let us not try to carry any part of hell with us to heaven. The two will not mix. Seek the life of Jesus Christ everywhere by living for yourself nowhere. Make him your joy and peace. Look to him to bring his life to bear in all your circumstances and trials. He will. "I have come that you might have life, and that you might have it abundantly" (John 10:10). This is his promise. This is the reality that God declares to us in his gospel. Let us praise him and seek to be found in Christ, to know him and the power of his resurrection, even the fellowship of his sufferings. If we suffer with him, it is so that we might reign with him forever, be with and like him, raised from the dead in glory, holiness, and love.

My Peace I Give to You

In the Upper Room Discourse, our Lord said to his disciples, "Peace I leave with you, my peace I give unto you" (John 14:27). "My peace" is astounding. His life was filled with labor, sorrow, and opposition. The cross ever loomed before him. The evil one tried to destroy him as soon as he was born. At the beginning of his public ministry, Satan directly assailed him with subtle temptations designed to overthrow him. As his public ministry matured, he said, "But I have a baptism to be baptized with, and how I am straitened till it be accomplished" (Luke 12:50: "How great is my distress until it is accomplished:" ESV). In the last week before his ordeal, he said, "Now is my soul troubled; and what shall I say? Father, save me from this hour? But for this cause came I unto this hour" (John 12:27).

How could the Man of Sorrows speak of "my peace?" Peace seems the last thing our Lord would claim to possess. He was so afflicted by his trial in the wilderness that angels were sent to revive him. In Gethsemane, angels returned lest he expire under the horrible anticipation of the cross. How much greater terrors must have afflicted him when he was actually struck down by the sword of divine justice? Yet, he speaks of "my peace." Peace must be something we can possess in the midst of the sorrow, pain, and the busiest of lives.

When we look for the source of our Lord's peace, let us begin with Psalm 16:8: "I have set the Lord always before me: because he is at my right hand, I shall not be moved." Jesus set his Father before him. He had a constant sense of carrying out his Father's will. Fellowship with his Father was the way he lived. He undertook nothing except at his Father's direction. More than any other who has ever lived, he could say: "All my ways are before thee" (Ps. 119:168). Luke especially emphasizes that our Lord prayed constantly. After many a busy day, he spent many sleepless nights seeking his Father. He lived and spoke in conscious awareness of his Father's nearness, which gave him calmness of spirit and resolution of purpose. Fellowship with his Father gave him indomitable peace amid his struggles for our salvation.

133

To this we must add his delight in his Father's will. Nothing pleased him more than obeying his Father. "I always do those things that please him" (John 8:29). Obedience was both fuel to his love and the fruit of his love for the Father (John 15:9-10). He came into the world with this purpose: "Lo, I have come, in the volume of the book it is written of me: I delight to do thy will, O my God: yea, thy law is within my heart" (Ps. 40:7-8). We must not miss the connection between righteousness and peace. "Great peace have they which love thy law: and nothing shall offend them [make them to stumble]" (Ps. 119:165). Peace is essentially the settled harmony we have when we are walking in trusting obedience to God. Sin disturbs our sense of peace with him and hinders our satisfaction in his glory. Peace is his smile felt by the obedient soul. Our Savior's peace was perfect because his obedience was perfect.

Deeper yet, he was submissive to his Father's will. Shall I not drink the cup the Father has given me (John 18:11)? He said this at the moment the soldiers came to arrest him in the garden. If there was ever a time to fight back, this would have been it. Yet, he had fought and won the battle of submission a few minutes earlier. "Not my will, but thine be done" (Luke 22:42). When the moment of crisis came, he was ready, at peace, unflinching in his purpose, able to command that whole chaotic scene so that not one of his sheep was lost. He would soon be in torments as the cup of our judgment was poured out upon him, but even then his flesh rested in hope (Ps. 16:9). At the end, his "It is finished" was the climax of his submission, a victory shout, a declaration of peace obtained for sinners, peace obtained through righteousness (John 19:30).

Taking our cue from these three foundations of his peace, we may say that our lack of peace is the fruit of too little fellowship with the Father, slight delight in doing his will, and resistance to his will. One may say, "Well, he was perfect, and I am not; what do you expect?" Our Savior fought for peace by fighting to obey. While he was sinless, he was not above temptation. His holiness was not passive but an active, constant resolution to be consecrated to his Father and to seek his Father's fellowship and help. As our Mediator, he learned obedience (Heb. 5:8).

134

Consider the wonder that he prayed. At one level, we might well question his need for prayer. Did he not have all the resources of heaven and earth at his disposal? Was he ever in need? The reality of his humanity forces itself upon our consideration. He humbled himself. Although he was "in the very form of God," everything that God was and had being his, he did not avail himself of his divine prerogatives but took the form of a servant. His peace, then, required that he live in our condition, become subject to our weakness, and drink deeply of our sorrows. It will not do to say that "I cannot be like Jesus." He became like us to make us like him.

How did our Lord respond to a busy life? He prayed continually. He meditated upon the Scriptures. He sought his Father in all seasons. His Father was his strength. He kept clearly before him the will of his Father. As we seek to walk with God, by remembering that "all our ways are before him," we shall enjoy this peace. It is the way Jesus gives us his peace. We can pray, for example, "Lord, I need peace," and the Lord says back to us, "Are you seeking the Father in prayer as I did? Are you casting your cares upon him? When you are tempted, do you call upon God for help as I did?" He has left us his peace by opening the way for his fellowship. He has opened heaven to us. We have his righteousness as our clothing, his name as our shield and identity, and his blood as our cleansing. The Holy God invites us to lay hold upon his throne of grace as our citadel of security.

Peace requires regular renewal. Our Savior's peace was constantly assaulted. His ministry began with Satan's mocking temptations of his baptismal anointing as the Son of God and Savior of sinners. Thereafter the pressure of duty and the weight of sorrows left him with few moments of external peace. The cross stalked his quiet moments. The fickle mob sought either to stone him or to make him its puppet king. What was his response in every season? He prayed. He remembered why he had come into the world. He resolved to obey his Father's will, whatever the personal cost.

The same must be true of us. We are "strangers and pilgrims." We shall find the going much as he did: constant vexations, ample

135

duty, and many sorrows. Life will not turn out as we anticipated. We shall find that our Lord did not exaggerate the disciple's cross. What then? Give up. Seek the broader path. No. Seek God. Then, Jesus Christ will give us his peace. It is one of the greatest gospel treasures he left to us. It is that for which the world seeks but can never find. Why is this? "God is not in all his thoughts" (Ps. 10:4). The world will not seek God, and therefore the world is consigned to a tumultuous existence. The wicked cannot rest; they cannot have true peace (Isa. 57:20-21).

Our destiny is different. Jesus gives his peace to us. I marvel that our Lord would be concerned with us at all. We deserve to be restless and disturbed. Sin has done this to us. Jesus Christ shows us the way to live this peace by setting God always before us, delighting to do his commands, and submitting ourselves to his will. Peace will not come in a day, but it will come. Jesus Christ came, obeyed, suffered, and died to secure our peace. He is our peace. Let us rejoice in him and be deeply humbled by his love. This is the first step to peace. He will carry us the rest of the way, for he gives his children the gift of his submission, the fruit of his obedience. "If any man thirsts, let him come to me and drink" (John 8:37).

If we would "set God always before us," we cannot be mushy-minded or averse to thinking. God is a speaking God and walking with him is inseparable from listening to him. The more of his word we have in our hearts and the more we meditate upon it, the more peace we shall have. To have peace, we must not imbibe the cheap grace mentality that is ravaging some corners of Christ's vineyard. False teachers set grace and obedience at odds, but God says that the way to enjoy the peace our Savior purchased for us with his blood is through obedience. The less concerned with obeying God we are, the less peace Jesus will give us.

We must not look for peace in escape – from our circumstances, the crying children, marriage difficulties, financial distress. Our Savior never ran away from trouble and service, nighttime prayer vigils, and ministering to every needy person who came his way. He knew that peace is God's benediction upon the soul that is submissive to his wise government of our lives. The more we chafe against rule over us, or complain about our circumstances, the less peace we shall have. God will not give it to us. He will teach us that he is our peace in the midst of our troubles.

When Jesus Loves Us

God's love is wiser than we can ever comprehend (Isa. 55:8-9). God's love rescued Abraham from Ur and then led him to wander as a stranger and pilgrim in the earth, wait decades for the child of promise, then yield his son to be sacrificed. Joseph and Jeremiah were loved by God, and they languished in dungeons and pits for obeying God. God loved Noah so much that in order to save him, he sealed him up in an ark that was more like a floating casket than anything else. David was beloved by God as a man after his own heart, but he spent many years as a vagabond on the run from Saul. Job, one of the holiest men who ever lived, was also the most tried and sifted, without any other explanation than I am the glorious God.

Nothing is more wonderful than to be loved by God. Yet, nothing is more absolutely humbling, often inexplicable, and sometimes deeply troubling. If he loves us, why does he allow us to suffer and to feel like we are going to suffocate under the weight of various trials?

Jesus loved Lazarus, and his two sisters, Mary and Martha (John 11:5). Beyond the redeeming, securing, eternal love that he shares with all his people, his heart was especially knit to a few. They were drawn to him more deeply than others, and he to them. Love begets love. He who would have Jesus Christ as a close friend must have an adoring, obedient, and trusting heart toward him. Peter, James, and John were also close to our Lord, with John specifically called "the beloved." The Lord shared with them alone his highest glories on the Mount of Transfiguration and his deepest agonies in the Garden of Gethsemane. He does not play favorites. Yet, he will not come to our house and abide with us if we are cold to him or keep him at arm's length (John 14:21-23; Rev. 3:20).

Mary and Martha sent word to Jesus that Lazarus was sick. The Lord did not go running to his friend. A thought from his holy, powerful mind would have healed Lazarus instantly. No such thought was forthcoming, no healing word from a distance, as in the case of the nobleman's son (John 4:50). Silence. He allowed two days to pass before informing his disciples that Lazarus had been sick and was now dead. In this interval, Mary and Martha were deeply grieving for their brother and longing for their Lord. He did not come. Their brother lay in the tomb. They knew Jesus loved him. Why did he not come? He could have spared them this bitterness.

Ponder carefully our Lord's silence and his delay. To his beloved friends, it seemed to be neglect and indifference. This was so unnecessary to their way of thinking. But when Jesus loves us, he does not give us what we want without first making our wants holy. His love does not prevent our tears, our suffering, even our death. Even when we call upon him, as Mary and Martha did, he does not answer us when and how we think he should or would – love on our terms. His love is pure and purifying, and this is exactly the reason he allows us to suffer. It is strange, but it is a fact. His love is wise. He knows what is best for us. His love is good. It always gives so much better than we can anticipate or understand in the midst of our tears and trials. Jesus did go to them – finally. His love is faithful. He will come when he is ready, often when the last wisps of hope are fluttering on the hoarse prayers of a tried faith.

When Jesus arrived, Martha ran to meet him. Her brother was dead; she desired her Lord. She trusted his glory and power. "Even now, whatsoever you will ask of God, God will give it to you" (John 11:22). She prefaced this with holy presumption – "If you had been here, my brother had not died" (v. 21). Here are love and faith wrestling with disappointment and perplexity. Already her faith is triumphant, overcoming through the pain and embracing the future by trusting the power and wisdom of her Lord. When Jesus says, "Your brother shall rise again," his words instill fresh strength in her. She lays holds of the hope of the resurrection of the dead. She is blessed to hear privately the most precious words that ever fell on mortal ear. "I am the resurrection, and the life: he that believes in me, though he were dead, yet shall he live" (v. 25).

Wise and holy is the love of our Savior. He led Martha away from her brother to him. Her brother was not what she needed most. She must believe and hold fast to the Lord of life; otherwise she would put more stock in Lazarus being with her than in Jesus's presence. Jesus was more necessary for her happiness than her brother. "Martha, do you believe this" (v. 26)? Her answer is a confession of faith that ranks with the highest ever uttered: "Yea, Lord: I believe that thou art the Christ, the Son of God, which should come into the world" (v. 27). You did not come and heal my brother, but I trust you. I grieve, but you will never fail me. You remain the Son of God: glorious, powerful, faithful. I now see that I received what I needed; you came. She has no idea of what is about to take place. She rests in hope that though Jesus did not heal Lazarus, he will one day raise him. Still grieving, she lays hold of the resurrection promise and rests contentedly in her Lord.

What follows is well known. Jesus stood before the tomb of his friend – shuddering in himself, facing the horrors of death, his coming sacrifice for sinners leering at him from the recesses of Lazarus' tomb. He prayed for the Father to glorify his name, and a voice from heaven like thunder answered him. "I have both glorified it and will glorify it again" (v. 28). Jesus proclaimed the downfall of Satan by his death. His own death would seem to contract his declaration, "I am the resurrection and the life." Nevertheless, his sacrifice of love and obedience removed our curse, brought an end to Satan's dark reign over the world of men, and broke the dominion of death. He stood before the tomb of Lazarus. He wept. The Giver of life was shaken to the depths of his holy soul by the deadly wages of our sin. He called Lazarus by name. Life called death to release its victim. Lazarus came forth.

In the end, Martha and Mary received their brother from the dead. This is the fairy tale ending to which we are selfishly inclined. This is when God loves us – when he gives us what we want. This is not love, else God is reduced to our personal genie. His love is much more marvelous than this. Jesus knows what is in our hearts (John 2:24-25), all the selfishness and earthbound affections that plague us. His love lifted Martha higher; it lifts us higher. When we cry and suffer loss, when we are weary with waiting, he leads us to see our true life. "I am the resurrection and the life." To be strong, faith must feed upon heartier bread than "everything turns out fine in the end"; or, "Well, it was tough, but I got what I wanted." I must eat the bread of life, Jesus Christ. I must rest contentedly in his wisdom and promise, in him as my only life.

Jesus does not bestow this bread in crumbs. Look at what the delay taught Martha. It led her to her Lord: to rest in his wisdom and trust his care. In the midst of her tears, his loving dealings with her brought her back to the confession that is better than loved-ones raised from the dead: "Thou art the Christ, the Son of God, which should come into the world." We can have everything we want, but without knowing Jesus as the Christ of God, it is nothing but a feast of dust. We can lose everything – health, security, liberty, children – but if we have the Son of God dwelling with us by his Spirit, life is a banquet of glory. It is better to cry with Jesus Christ than to laugh without him. It is better to lose everything else but to have him than to have everything else without him. Other thick slices of living bread he gave to them that day before raising Lazarus, love they would never have known had he not died: that precious saying, "I am the resurrection"; Jesus' wondrous prayer and proclamation of victory; his tears before Lazarus' tomb, which showed that he entered far more deeply into their sorrows than they imagined; his mighty voice restoring Lazarus to life. Love showed them glory – the glory of God in the face of Jesus Christ.

Our Lord would show us that same glory in our sufferings and sorrows. See my hand in them, he says. Trust me, no matter what you see with your eyes. I am more powerful than death, or pain, tragedy, hunger, and conflict. I am the Lord; beside me there is no other. And I love you. The goal of Jesus' love is far higher than to make it all better. One day, he will make everything better, but we must first be transformed. He begins this work now. He shows us glory – through the tears, in the tears. He sustains us when we seem to be gasping the last breath of faith. He shows us that it is better to be loved by him than anything else in the world.

The Hem of His Garment

We have a sad tendency to read the gospel narratives as holy relics of a cherished past. We are thankful to have them and are occasionally aroused to protect our collection from wolves. Yet, like relics and mementos, they often lie beautifully stored and carefully preserved, but merely possessed and taking up space without fulfilling the vital purpose for which they were given to us. Let us once, however, admit their inspiration and enter fully into their purpose, they become the flaming presence of Jesus Christ in our lives. Being inspired, they are the living voice of the Holy Spirit, whose words never fall to the ground lifeless.

Even more, they are Christ's autobiography, for he sent his Spirit to give them to us and preserve them for us. To this indisputable truth must be added another. The Gospels are the way our Savior would have us understand and relate to him. His word is as living and powerful as he is (Col. 3:16; Heb. 4:12). Through his word he is present with us and would have us seek and possess his presence. Therefore, as we read, believe, and obey his word, our Savior comes to his believing Church in each generation, saving, challenging, and transforming us, even as he did his original hearers and witnesses.

The Gospels are historical; they are our Savior's actual words and deeds. This is far more than a dogma that must be defended against prejudiced critics. The Gospels are the way our Savior walks and talks with us, saves and rules over us, encourages and loves us. Many centuries separate us from the first accomplishment of his deeds recorded therein. Because of his promise to abide with us forever, no centuries and no distance separate us from the same exalted Savior who now reigns at the right of the Father. He does the same powerful works for us and says the same words that are "spirit and life." To have Jesus Christ, then, we must live in his Gospels, for he lives there, still speaks there, still works there. If we use the Gospels as he intends, we may touch and draw near to him there, in all his saving glory and power, friendship and warmth, transcendence and nearness.

A nobleman came to Jesus and asked him to come to his house to raise his dead daughter to life. Jesus said he would come, for he is ever the enemy of death. They begin moving through the crowds that ever surrounded our Lord; though most did not believe in him, they could not but be drawn to him, even as the seas could not but respond to their Maker. They press upon him, calling out to him, watching his every move, waiting for anything to fall from his lips. He stops. Someone has touched him. "Who touched me" (Luke 8:45)? Looking around, Peter is incredulous. "Who touched you, Lord? Everyone is touching you." No, someone touched me. It is not every touch or approach to Jesus that is a touch of true faith, obtains the object of its desire, and benefits from the encounter with the Son of God.

A woman lies prostrate at Jesus' feet. What a miserable creature she was! Suffering from a lengthy, embarrassing, and isolating disease, she had thought to herself, Matthew records, that if she could but touch the hem of his garment, she would be made whole. All her resources had been exhausted upon potential cures; all her hopes had been dashed. Here, however, was one of the daughters of the ancient faith, like Ruth seeking a covering at Boaz's feet. To speculate on her mental and emotional state will only obscure the one certainty: she knew that the Son of God could heal her.

How, though, could she approach him? Her condition was too delicate to permit a direct approach, for this would undoubtedly result in bringing her misery to public view, a thought too uncomfortable for her to contemplate. A private interview might bring the desired cure, but would Jesus' disciples allow a woman with such a disease to approach him alone? Should she shout after him? Long seclusion due to the ceremonial uncleanness associated with this disease made her averse to anything that would draw unwelcome attention. She saw the thronging crowds. Ah, here she would remain unnoticed. So, reaching the dense mass around him, she began inching closer, likely stooping or crawling through the jumbled mass of bodies, for it is said that she reached out to touch the hem of his garment, its extremity or border.

The Hem of His Garment

The sensation of healing was immediate. Knowing that healing power had left him, that faith had touched him, Jesus turned, looked upon the woman. Trembling, she came forward and confessed before all that she had touched him, the reasons, and the result. "Daughter, be of good comfort: thy faith hath made thee whole; go in peace" (v. 48). By these words, Jesus healed her inwardly, releasing her from the dark grip of despair, the reign of frustration and isolation, the paralysis of loneliness and fear. O, the virtue of touching Jesus is always holistic, never piecemeal, always beyond our assessment of our need, never limited to the weakness of our faith.

Man is ever tenacious in the pursuit of the object of his desire. It is a great tragedy, however, that these desires are often deadly to his soul. Obtaining his desire, he gains great harm and misery (Ps. 106:15). His condition is worse for the possession. Let the desire be good, though exceedingly difficult to obtain, and even the pursuit is ennobling. How much more when our desire is for Jesus Christ, the wisdom, righteousness, and power of God? Learn, then, from this unnamed daughter of Zion, that all your desire must be toward him.

Whoever you may be or think yourself to be, apart from him, her condition is yours. You have spent all your resources to procure your desire, even assuming its legitimacy. Without Jesus, "without avail" is the result of your efforts. You have struggled with relationships, inner sins, and family duties. You may, like her, suffer from a longstanding or painful disease. There may be one sin, one duty, or one dream that wholly occupies the horizon of desire; you have been frustrated in its pursuit or devastated by its realization. You seek fulfillment, deliverance, or purpose. Put all other thoughts aside but this: whatever is worth having, it is to be found only in the Son of God, for he is the life and light of the world. All else is death and darkness. If you have him, he possesses you unto joy unspeakable and full of glory. If you do not have him, life is but a dreary shadow. How may you obtain him, without whom all else is empty and meaningless?

A passing thought or two will never bring you to Jesus. You may have grown up in the church and know a great deal about him.

Knowledge about Jesus without desire for Jesus is a barren wasteland, a desert of dissatisfying arrogance, coldness of soul, and bitterness toward God and others. You may seek religious experiences, closeness with others that seem to be closer to him than you are, or fuller book knowledge. These never substitute for Jesus himself as the object of our desire, for seeking him with your whole heart. All else must be abandoned to obtain this pearl; the secrets of the inner life exposed; the idols of the heart forsaken. You must seek him: even if but to touch the hem of his garment. He will give you more; he will give himself to you in all his fullness. Often weak, faith cannot apprehend the magnificence of his grace and generosity. How should you approach him?

There is only one way. He must seek you. It is true that this gospel woman came to Jesus, but we must ask why. She had heard of him. The thoughts of acting as she did would never have occurred to her in her emptiness and isolation had some whisper of his words and works not reached her ear, had Jesus not called to her through them. Jesus granted her a germ of faith to come. Like Nathaniel under the fig tree, Jesus knew this woman long before she came to him. He knew her soul in adversity. He anticipated her coming. He empowered her coming. She responded by coming.

The exalted Son of Man is similarly calling us through his words and works. Done and said long ago, they were, but they are still living and breathing in the Gospels – not a dim echo through the millennia, not a faint glimmer of glory. He shines as brightly in them now as he did then. He lives through them, in them, imparting himself to us through them. Will you cling to him through them? Will you hold the Gospels as relics or sources of doctrine, or will you come to Jesus as this woman did? She heard of the very deeds and words of which we read in our Gospels. She came. Drawn by Jesus, she reached toward him in her infirmity, her embarrassment, her utterly emptied condition. She was made whole by her faith – not a mystical touch, not a mountaintop experience, but by a humble believing that Jesus Christ was who his words and works proclaimed him to be: the Son of God and Savior of sinners. She put all else aside, even her last hiding place of personal dignity and self-respect. All is worth sacrificing that I might touch him.

Is this your heart? You may sit in church services all your life and never touch Jesus. You may know a great deal about him but never be touched by him. Or, you may waste your life pursuing one illusive dream after another, but receive a blighted soul as your reward, and that even if your pursuits do not take you into the dark dens of depravity but consist in things otherwise good and necessary. Without seeking Jesus, without desiring him, without coming to him in the light of his words and works, you will remain isolated and empty, nursing bitterness, filled with self-loathing.

Although we were made for God, we gave up this pursuit in favor of Satan's lies. Fallen human nature is unchanged these six millennia. Only if we are remade by his touch, by his saving grace, dying love, and resurrection power will we ever realize the purpose of our creation. Come to him. Believe him to be as his word declares: the healer of man's uncleanness. Believe him able to do as his works reveal: restoring and forgiving men, reconciling them to God, raising up the dead and blind to reign with him. Believe his promise to be with us. Believe that he gives himself to us afresh each day through his Gospels, as we believe and meditate upon them, relate to him as they direct us, and trust in him alone.

Reach out to him, even if you find in yourself all manner of vileness and weakness; even if you have, you think to yourself, thrown your life and opportunities away on trifles and vanities; even if but to touch the hem of his garment. And finding him, do not let go. It is all his work, and nothing of ourselves, but he has spoken God's words and done his Father's works as so many invitations to us to touch him, to taste and see, to believe and live. He will not turn you away if you look to him. He will satisfy and heal, restore and empower, encourage and motivate. He will say to you as he said to the healed woman, "Be of good comfort; go in peace."

Would you have fresh supplies of his power? Renewed courage and zeal? Would you be delivered from a besetting sin, made more constant in his service, quickened in love and thankfulness? These, too, are found only in coming to Jesus, like this woman, reaching out to him, touching him, believing that he has lost none of the love and compassion, grace and power, wisdom and goodness that he shows us in the Gospels. Is not this the very hope of a recovered church and converted world? That we might again touch the hem of his garment, that God-given faith may again set its affections on things above, where Christ is, seated in glory and power, goodwill and compassion? The same malady that affects us individually is dreadfully debasing the bride of Christ: too much reaching out to the world, too much dependence upon earthly means and methods, too little seeking of Jesus Christ.

His touch alone heals. His voice alone raises the dead. He came to bring us into the holy circle of love, joy, and obedience (John 15:9-11). We learn this and much more in his Gospels. Through them, at this very moment, he offers himself to us. What are you crawling toward? What is the object of your desire? Make it Jesus Christ, as he reveals himself in his Gospels. Believe his promises, depend upon his power and love, and he shall grant you everything else you require. When faith touches the hem of his garment, it receives life, righteousness, peace, and holiness from him. It receives him.

Speaking of Jesus

Some years ago I knew a Christian who was always speaking of Jesus. I do not mean that he was incapable of conversation on other subjects, socially backward, or a religious fanatic. He was a man's man, loved the outdoors, met no strangers, and feared nothing. No, it is simply that he loved to speak of our Lord. Conversations about other things he interwove with Jesus' works, words, and promises respecting that particular subject. Even around those whom he felt to be true believers, he was always asking questions like, "What is Jesus doing in your life?" "Have you had an opportunity to share him with others?" "Are you seeking the Lord?" I am especially struck by the memory of his oft-used question: "Isn't Jesus wonderful?"

I realize now that his speaking of Jesus, though it sometimes made me a bit uncomfortable, is the way we ought to be talking all the time. Whatever subject one wishes to discuss, whatever world problem, family need, or personal failure is pressing upon us, Jesus is the way, the truth, and the life. If he is not brought into the conversation, if, indeed, he is not the Lord of the conversation, then words, time, and opportunity have been wasted.

I have sensed, though, that even among believers, there is a reticence to speak of Jesus. Perhaps we feel it is too personal to speak publicly of his dealings with us. Other subjects are always fighting for our words. Then again, you may have known someone who was always talking about Jesus, the Lord, or the Bible, and it left you uncomfortable. People just do not talk like this, you thought to yourself, and it impressed you that speaking of Jesus so openly and constantly is a little strange. We know about Jesus. We believe the gospel. There is no point in talking about things everyone already understands. Not talking about Jesus with fellow-believers is a likely sign that you find it difficult if not impossible to do so around unbelievers. The heart is generally consistent in the subjects it prefers to discuss or not discuss, and speaking of Jesus cannot be turned off and on like a light switch.

There are other reasons that we may not regularly speak of Jesus. Any discussion of Jesus must inevitably turn to his sacrifice

148

on the cross. This is a stumbling block, sometimes even to the believer, for any regular discourse about him must necessarily involve being humbled before his cross, considering it our delight, our boast, our tree of life. All power to do anything good and pleasing to God comes from the cross, for by it "the world has been crucified to me, and I to the world" (Gal. 6:14). Any real power to love, forgive, and do flows from his pierced side. Hence, speaking of Jesus means that we are humbled before that cross – not once, occasionally, or when we feel especially guilty. Before the cross is the Christian way of life. If we do not meditate upon his redeeming love and glory in his cross, it is hardly to be expected that we will have the humility required for speaking of Jesus.

Consider the apostles prior to the death and resurrection of Jesus Christ as proof that even believers can be embarrassed by the cross, that pride can take such deep root in us that we do not have the desire to speak of our Lord. Every time the Lord Jesus mentioned that he must suffer and die, Peter, serving as their spokesman, rebuked him. O, they were all quite willing to hear about reigning with Jesus, especially since they conceived of this as exchanging places of power with the Romans. Miracles, refuting detractors, and feeling as if you have all the answers – these topics were pleasant. They required no personal humility; indeed, they could and did feed their pride.

Something happened to these men after Jesus' death and resurrection – they could not but speak the things they had seen and heard. They went everywhere preaching Christ and him crucified and raised. Why? The cross of Christ is the stake in the heart of pride. If you have been before that cross, if you live before that cross, it cannot but be your boast, your joy, your greatest amazement. Yes, Jesus did many wonderful things besides die for us, and his word is very broad in its themes and applications, but they must eventually return to the cross. All wisdom to understand, power to do, life to feel, strength to persevere, and joy to suffer come only from the crucified One, who showed us the way to the crown by bearing the cross.

Within our relationships, to consider a more immediate example, we are tempted to be relationally ambitious, i.e., to have the final say, to be the known expert on a given subject, to appear to have everything under control. Yet, where ego reigns, it is rare for there to be any sincere speaking of Jesus, even among believers. Then, there is the tendency for us to be drawn together more out of common interests – parenting, sports, hobbies, political persuasions, jobs – than in common love for Jesus. Yes, it is there, somewhere, but it is pushed to the margins of our talking because he has been pushed to the margins of our lives. This is especially true when believers have spent a good deal of time together, understand each other's foibles and eccentricities, and migrate toward comfortable relationships in which the sheer delight of speaking of Jesus is uncomfortable with those who know you well.

There is one reason at the root of all the others, and it is also the narrow path leading back to speaking of Jesus. We simply have lost any sense of his presence, the importance of self-consciously thinking of him, and – wonder of all wonders – that he is thinking warmly of us, walking with us, working in us, ruling over all things for our sake. We talk about things that are important to us. If we are walking with Jesus Christ, he will be the most important thing in our lives. We will begin to look at the "little things" – the small victories, the daily evidences of his presence and power, the times he lifts us up from the miry pit – as worth sharing, for we desire him to be "exalted and extolled very high."

His word, as we walk with him, becomes more than the religious thought for the day, like the daily platitude on the desk calendar or internet site. His word is felt to be, as it is whether or not we feel it, his voice, calling us out of the tomb, giving the new creation each new day, opening our blind eyes each morning to the splendor of his smiling face. His word then burns within us, like in the hearts of the two that walked with Jesus. The answers to prayer we receive, far from being the expected return for telling God our wish list, are evidences that he is truly the high priest over the house of God, who sympathizes with us in our weakness, who is saving us to the uttermost as we come unto God through him.

These things cannot be held within our hearts. They are not our private treasure, something that gives us personal confirmation that all is well. They belong to the whole body of Christ, indeed, to the world. They must be shared for he must be glorified.

Thus, when we think of our witness-bearing function and responsibility in the world, what else is this but an extension of the speaking of Jesus that is the fruit of walking with him, delighting in his cross, and adoring him in his glory? We can take apologetics classes and learn methods; this will not make us any more willing to speak of Jesus. Guilt never motivates, at least for long. Speaking of Jesus – naturally, personally, humbly – is the fruit of being in his society – regularly, personally, and adoringly. Understanding the times and knowing the beliefs and arguments of unbelievers will not make you ready to give an answer or compelling when you do – only a heart that truly loves the Lamb of God, sees his cross as going always before us, as well as his empty tomb, glorious reign, and promised presence, will make us anxious to speak of Jesus to the lost. The same Christ before whose cross we are bowing and in whose life-giving presence we are delighting must become their Christ, if God should be pleased to use our humble and adoring testimony to his grace and mercy. And when does he usually draw men to the Savior? When we are speaking of Jesus in the course of daily life, for his word is his power unto salvation.

Speaking of Jesus does not mean that we are always reciting John 3:16. It does not mean we cannot talk of other things, enjoy other activities, or be vitally concerned about other issues. It means that we see them in all their relation to him. He must have his part in every conversation, not only as his right but also because he is the delight and very life of the believing soul. It is constantly drawn back to him in its words and thoughts by a reflex of love and grace, wonder and thankfulness.

~5~
Transforming Glory

Christ Transforming

In times of perceived decay or crisis, men crave the new. If something is new, it must be better. If the old had worked, we would not need the new. Thus, we have various emergent-isms, the "new Calvinism" (which is really not new and not really Calvinism), and new ways of worship. Novelty's parade will not, however, reduce the weight of the disciple's cross, make unbelieving men any friendlier to the gospel, or better enable us to overcome sin. New spirituality is like a new model year for automobiles. It generates PR and gives bored consumers something to talk about, but the newness wears off. The most relevant things are the most quickly irrelevant.

Only the old ways will work. God has said so. "Thus saith the Lord, Stand ye in the ways, and see, and ask for the old paths, where is the good way, and walk therein, and ye shall find rest for your souls. But they said, We will not" (Jer. 6:16). Many today say to God and his old paths, "We will not." We need excitement, to feel like we are part of something new, to reach men who will not follow the old ways. They will not work for electronic souls. They are too hard, require too much thought and have too few changing scenes. Our churches will stay small. No, we prefer the new. God will understand. We are being led by the Spirit and feel good about what we are doing, so it must be from the Lord.

The reason we run after shiny new things is that the old has lost his newness to our hearts. Notice what Jesus Christ says of himself: I am "the same yesterday, today, and forever" (Heb. 13:8). The same? Yes, he does not change, but his changelessness is never sterile or uninteresting. He is alive, possesses unsearchable riches of love and grace, wisdom and knowledge, and is ever building his Church – so that she will stay faithful to the old ways. Of himself, he says: "Behold, I make all things new" (Rev. 21:5). He never loses the "dew of his youth" (Ps. 110:3), the first flush of youth's strength and potential. He was dead, but he is alive forevermore. He has life, fullness of life, living waters that never cease flowing.

Christ Transforming

When we feel the need for something new, we need to take a closer look at the old. Consider a congregation that wants to grow or simply feels that it has grown stagnant. Many options are available to generate fresh enthusiasm. Instead, we should return to the old that is ever new. We should become more serious about prayer, specifically praying for the Lord to quicken us by his Spirit, give us a heart for his word, and strengthen us unto holiness. We should pray the old gospel promises, pray to be made truly gospel men and women in our homes and workplaces, and pray for the Lord to work in our midst. If we take him seriously here, he will transform us. There will be less bickering and stale worship and more joy in our Savior. He will give us these blessings if we ask. We will disciple one another and engage one another about Jesus Christ, his cross and reign, his work in our lives. We will be invigorated and thus able to encourage one another. Since his full life and gifts and graces are shared not with any one believer but with the whole body, then the more we are with his people the more we shall learn of him and grow in him. This is the old way. It is the Christ way.

The growth that comes from Christ transforming us will not be on our schedule. When he grows in us, that growth will be a bit uncomfortable. In transforming, he breaks down the old sinful thought patterns and habits. He challenges us through his word and through one another. The old way is truly Christ in us, Christ transforming us into his image. The old ways will soon lose their oldness, for our ever fresh Savior is walking this way. When we are serious about him, about discipleship, about his word, praying always with all prayer and supplication with thanksgiving, the living Savior comes down by his Spirit and quickens and renews us.

The old ways are the most extraordinary ways. Men do not like them because they place us on a path that is not under our control and cannot be neatly measured. But do we want Jesus Christ? We must come after him on the old paths. He is where his word and sacraments are, where his people are praying with humble hearts, and where each disciple is seeking to live unto the Lord. A congregation that believes and lives this way will grow. It will grow up into Christ; he will grow in it. It will love. It will worship. The word of Christ will grow and multiply.

Consider, Christian man, your desire for your family to be more joyful in the Lord, love and serve one another more faithfully, and have sufficient domestic discipline so that after doing all that is necessary to lead a family, energy and desire remain to worship, pray, and serve in the Lord's living temple. You have likely learned that new rules will not accomplish this. Nor will your complaining against your wife or ordering everyone around. But Jesus Christ will transform your home. He usually begins by transforming you.

Begin by committing your family to the Lord (Ps. 37:5). Commit to praying for your wife and children each day, especially praying that the Lord will remember his covenant promises. Confess your headship sins: not praying for your children as you have vowed to do, impatience, not teaching your family the Lord's expectations from his word, and not providing loving discipline and encouragement to live unto him. Repent of your sins, the many holes in your umbrella of headship and protection, your provocations of the Lord, your selfishness. Turn from them to God and his word, from sin to righteousness. Trust the blood of Jesus Christ as your cleansing, his intercession as your unconquerable hope and help.

Then, commit yourself to be guided by the Lord, truly living unto him in your home: the way you talk to your wife or children – does it sound like Jesus or an army sergeant? When was the last time you encouraged with calmness or wiped a tear with tenderness? Take the lead in picking up, washing dishes, but do not hold it up to your wife as if you are some kind of hero or martyr. Be a joyful servant. Be like Jesus. You can be like him only if you are seeking his grace and strength each day. Ask him for specific help where you need it. Do not stop asking. It will take time for your family to notice the difference, but Jesus Christ transforms men, even those who have a bad track record and years of neglect of the means of grace. He will do it.

Christ Transforming

The main issue with Christ transforming is trusting Christ. Will he really change me? How can he change me? This sin, or that habit, or this struggle has lasted for so long. Let us turn our eyes upon Jesus. He died, rose again, and reigns to reconcile sinners to God (Col. 1:21). He works in his children in order to present us "holy and unblameable and unreprovable in his sight" (v. 22). He will do this. Sin, poor training, and entrenched sin are no hindrances to him. He will make us holy before God.

He transforms as we continue in the old paths: "if ye continue in the faith grounded and settled, and be not moved away from the hope of the gospel" (v. 23). And here is the mystery of the gospel, the truth once veiled but now preached to us when Jesus Christ is preached to us: "Christ in us, the hope of glory" (v. 27). When we believe the gospel, cast ourselves upon Jesus Christ, and commit to following him, he dwells with us by his Spirit. He strengthens by his power, encourages us, renews us. He is present with us. We must not think of ourselves apart from Christ, or Christ apart from us. He is our Head and Savior, our Mediator and Lord. He is one with us, and we with him. His abiding presence will transform us. He will make us new.

As we believe upon his name, call upon his name, and continue trusting him, Jesus Christ dwells with us. Believe. Trust. Do not doubt. With Jesus Christ, all things are possible. We can do all things through his strength in us. This is the old path. We need nothing new but simply to follow the old, narrow way of walking with Jesus. Is this not the disciple's path? Why do we call ourselves Christians? It is because we are committed to him. "If any man will come after me" was his call. Come after him, child of God. Continue coming. Do not doubt for one moment that he will transform you. He is the Christ, the Son of the living God. He will not be frustrated or disappointed in his great work of renewing all the children of God into his beautiful image.

Broken in the Wilderness

I am often surprised by the Lord's disappointing my expectations. I think I will be able to get to work, for example, once everything is quiet, especially two rambunctious little boys. Quiet comes, but I cannot settle down to work. Or, if I look down the road of life to a time when there are not quite so many responsibilities – but that time will never come, at least while God gives me strength. It seems that we are always hoping for that pot of gold at the end of the rainbow. When my health returns, then I will be happy and productive; if I had more money, then I would be hospitable and serve others.

The life of Jesus comes to mind. He had no place to lay his head. Although he was surrounded with followers, most hated him. For three years, his closest friends did not understand him, sometimes resisted him, and finally fled from him. In his hour of agony in Gethsemane, he asked for their prayers, and they fell asleep. On the cross, he was stripped of all dignity and crucified as a common criminal. I have no doubt that many of those who jeered at him had known his healing touch.

And yet, in his poverty, weakness, and rejection, he obeyed his Father, prayed without ceasing, and saved the world. He looked at the world, personal limitations, and hard circumstances very differently than we do. He was always saying strange things to our way of thinking. "Take the lowest seat at the feast." "Wash one another's feet." Love your enemies." "Take no thought for tomorrow." What did he know that we resist learning?

God typically blesses, accomplishes great things, and enjoys fellowship with the laughably weak: Joseph in the dungeon, David and Goliath, Daniel in the lions' den, Elijah on Carmel. Again and again, God says to us, "You have no strength, but you do not need any. You only need me."

Here is the lesson. When we are weak, if we trust God and wait upon him (Isa. 40:31), we become strong. If we trust our brains, our experiences, our wealth, or anything else, he will bring us to moments of painful realization, as he did Peter. He leaves us to our own strength. See how that works out for you – not vindictively but a loving Father wooing us away from self to trust him. When you are ready to face the truth about yourself, that you are weaker than you know, more sinful than you can imagine, then you are in a position to be blessed and used.

Moses is a wonderful example of this. Around the age of forty, he ventured out from Pharaoh's household to visit his countrymen. Contrary to the usual movie dramatics, he knew he was a Hebrew. He saw an Egyptian taskmaster beating one of his countrymen, so he killed him and hid his body in the sand. The next day, he tried to make peace between two of his countrymen. He thought they would respect him as the deliverer of his people. They jeered at his pretensions and brought up the killing of the Egyptian. He ran away in fear into the wilderness – for forty years. He was the deliverer, but God would not use him as long as he trusted his own wisdom and strength. He had to be broken.

This should remind us of Jesus' statement. "He that exalts himself will be abased" (Luke 14:11). This little line overturns the whole philosophy of the world and crushes our delusions of strength. God is our only strength. We are slow to believe this. Moses' hard experience is typical for all those whom God uses, from the father with his family to the general on the battlefield. You have no strength, he says to us. I love you, but you must learn to trust me. You must learn to distrust yourself. You must also learn to rejoice in your weakness (2 Cor. 12:9), or you will never seek me or be strong.

Every Christian must do his time in the wilderness. For some like Moses, Elijah, and John, it is a real wilderness. For Joseph, it was a dungeon, David a sheepfold, and Paul the desert of Arabia. Sometimes the wilderness humbling lasts many years; for others like Peter, it is one night of racked conscience and fifty days of waiting for the Spirit. For a father, it is his daily closet time before the Lord, pleading God's promises and confessing his sins. For the mother, it is seeking strength to guide children, asking for submission to a weak husband, and perhaps looking to Jesus to be contented in a lonely place in her pilgrimage. For young adults, it is submission to parents and earnestly serving the Lord while single (1 Cor. 7:34). Every believer must pass through the wilderness, for every believer must be brought to the place where he says, "I am utterly empty of strength. Lord, unless you take me by the hand, uphold me by your strength, and guide me, I will instantly go astray."

Afflictions and trials are God's usual wilderness. Daily inconveniences, burdens, and frustrated expectations are the ways he breaks us. A season of indulged sin can be a wilderness, if in it God shows us our true selves and breaks our will so that our one desire becomes to do his will. Old age is a final pass through the wilderness to bring us back to childlike submission and to ripen us for heaven. Wives and mothers must especially pass through the wilderness of sifting and consecration. They must learn that neither husbands nor children can fill their hearts with lasting happiness – only Jesus can. They learn, even more than men, in a thousand ways, "My happiness is yielding to God." No one is exempt. All have to pass through the fire.

God's wilderness goal is quite simple. It is found in putting two statements of Scripture side by side, and then adding a third to drive the point home. The first is John 15:5: "Without me, ye can do nothing." The second is Philippians 4:13: "I can do all things through Christ which strengthens me." The final one is 2 Corinthians 12:9: "For my strength is made perfect in weakness." Meditate upon these together. They contain the glorious dynamic of faithful, Christ-centered living.

The first stresses our abysmal weakness. Forget the grand things. We cannot endure traffic patiently, or squawking children, or too many bills all at once, or prolonged sickness. We are nothing but weakness. Nothing. Sin has raped us of strength. The sooner we embrace this, the better, for until we do, there can be no progress and no peace.

The second stresses Christ's infinite strength, but it must follow the first. We trust, experience, and boast in Christ's strength only after he has broken us. Then, looking at whatever he places before us, he teaches us to say, "Lord, I cannot, but you can. This is too hard for me, but nothing is too hard for you. I wish this would go away, but I do not want to run from you or miss what you have for me. I will submit to you." We truly can do all things through Christ strengthening us. No sin or temptation is too strong for him. No daily burden is too heavy for him to carry. No disease is too ravaging. No lost opportunity, rejection, or loneliness is too bitter. He delivers the broken. He strengthens the weak who come to him in honest, humble faith.

The third says, "When I am broken and humbled before the Lord, I can expect him to do great things for me. In fact, he has sent the very things I want him to take away in order to empty me of me and fill me with him. His power rests upon me when I learn to accept what he brings into my life without groaning or complaining."

The various wildernesses through which we pass are no accident. We can ask the Lord to remove them, as Paul did his affliction, but our wise Savior says, "No. I want you to be strong in my strength. If I make all your problems go away or heal all your diseases, you would stop crying and trusting. You would only become weak and miserable again. No, it is better for you to remain bruised and broken. I will perfect you later. Now, however, I want my power to rest upon you. This will only happen if I keep you in the wilderness."

Certainly our Lord gives us seasons of joy. When he refreshes us with his love and grace, we forget the wilderness temporarily, for he is so refreshing! Heaven is really where he is. Still, we are weak and have not yet reached our heavenly inheritance, so there is a sense in which he keeps us in the wilderness – searching, seeking, hoping. For Moses and only a very few of the Israelites did their wilderness experience point them to Jesus and lead them to heaven. For the vast majority, it embittered and killed them, for they wanted life not on God's terms but on their own. If we are truly broken in the wilderness, we shall trust God's promise of strength and not complain against his wise providences. We must keep looking to our Good and Faithful Shepherd. He knows the way home and the best paths to take. He knows that there is no crown without the cross, no glory without suffering, no heaven without wilderness.

You Did It unto Me

His final coming to perfect his kingdom gave great strength to our Lord as he walked toward the cross. So heavy did that hour weigh upon him that he kept the full glory of his work ever before him. All of Isaiah 53 drove him: his humiliation and exaltation, his death and the "pleasure of the Lord shall prosper in his hand." The cross stood starkly in his path, but that was not the only thing that occupied his attention. Nor is it all that should occupy ours.

After discipling the nations, gathering his church in holiness, truth, and unity (John 17), and putting all the nations beneath his feet (1 Cor. 15:25; Heb. 10:12-13), he will return in glory. He would have us prepare for this hour, as well as to labor for it. With the cross looming before him, he told the Parable of the Talents (Matt. 25:14-30). We are to think of the gifts, graces, and opportunities he gives to us from heaven, his "traveling into a far country" (v. 14), as the spoils of his victory over sin and Satan by his death, resurrection, and ascension to heaven. He is still traveling there, for he has not yet returned.

Until he returns, we are to serve him. Notice that the "talents" he places into our hands are to be used and developed. We are only the custodians of what belongs to him. Be it business, music, family, and science – gifts that pertain to this life – or the higher spiritual gifts he has given us for the beautification and holiness of his Church, such as mercy, giving, governing, and teaching, all gifts are from him. To bury them in the dirt out of fear or laziness will bring his condemnation. He expects what he gives to be used faithfully and zealously. Whether he gives us one, three, or five talents, we are to go out and earn more with them. We do this by consecrating our lives to him, seeing our lives as nothing but an unfolding of his life and power in us, and working diligently to honor him who has given us everything.

There will be an accounting, an audit of our lives. This is discomforting; looking to Jesus, it is also very motivating, even exciting. He will perform the audit to reveal what he has done in us! We often make excuses. "I can only do so much; if I only had this or that; if only my family, finances, and friends were better than they are – then I would really do more." The Lord has given us these circumstances and opportunities. He calls us to improve them, stand where he has called us, even to grow there. This is impossible unless we are persuaded that we are serving the King and call upon him with faith and hope for help and wisdom. He who gave the gifts will help you in your use of them if you love and trust him.

His strictness is not to be missed. He did not correct the lazy servant for calling him a "hard man, reaping where you have not sown, and gathering where you have not strewn" (v. 24). We are to fear our Savior with adoring awe, "serve him with fear and rejoice with trembling" (Ps. 2:11). He was not lazy; nor shall we be, if we are in him, his true servants. He has given us a kingdom of graces and talents. We are to "occupy until he comes" (Luke 19:13), to extend his work and influence, even to pursue ardently those "greater works" he promised and empowers from the Father's right hand (John 14:12). This King permits no excuses: "Lord, I said 'grace, grace' all the time; Lord, I was a son and did not think I needed to take sin and righteousness, faithfulness and duty so seriously; Lord, I listened to some preachers who said everyone would enter into your kingdom as long as they were sincere in what they believed and accepting of others."

Cheap grace without responsibility and sonship without duty has cut the life-chord of diligent, serious, and joyful service to our Lord. "Grace" has become a mantra to excuse laziness and worldliness, even the flaunting of sin. "Sonship" is often twisted to deny any mature, watchful sense of accountability to God for his grace. This precious truth is in danger of becoming a receiving of his grace in vain (2 Cor. 6:1). Our Lord is exacting because he is an ever-present Savior who lovingly invites us to come to him for strength and kindly shepherds us. He takes himself seriously – his love, power, grace, cross, throne, and life in us – so he takes his work in us seriously. With such abundance of promised help, such a clear revelation of his will in the completed Scriptures, and such a wondrous indwelling presence of his Spirit, we are not permitted to bury his talent in the ground through sloth. We may not be cold in heart or negligent in duty toward the One who loved and gave himself for us.

Our Lord goes further to impress these truths upon us (Matt. 25:31-46). So deep and personal are his next words that it is difficult to take them into our hearts as fully as we should. Leaving the realm of parable – which, you will recall, he often told not to make plain the truth but to hide it from unbelieving hearts (Matt. 13:13) – he speaks of history, future history, your history and mine. When he returns from his glorious far country at the right hand of the Father, he will gather all the nations before him. In an instant, he will divide them, for he knows the heart of each man and nation. Sheep and goats will be the only two sides: no hazy grey, no uncertain purgatories, no line for nice people. The standard of judgment is straightforward: "Did you minister to me?" He speaks of food and drink, prison and sick visits – to me.

The righteous sheep will be speechless at the kingdom given to them, surprised by the approbation of the King (vv. 37-39). There is a certain self-forgetfulness when the heart is intent on serving Jesus. Love wants no cameras rolling when it cooks a meal or gives a coat to a needy brother. It needs none; pleasing its Lord is enough. He loves us; we love him. It is enough. Those talents we receive and develop: done for him, to please him, with him in mind. In fact, he does it, for all the fruits and gifts and graces are his life in us (Phil. 1:11). We can take no credit; if our heart is right, we want none. No productions, high drama, or websites required. We really do not want others to know. The right hand hides from the left, knowing its love to be such a dim reflection of his love that it is hardly worth the name. Our brothers need not know every time we pray for them. We are poor and sick with them, sharing only the talent the Lord has given us. It is his. We are his. We want only him. We love him.

The King's "unto me" is very important (v. 40). It screams: "Lord, I never thought myself much, did not mind high things, and was unconcerned about keeping up appearances before men. I only wanted you. You are very real to me; my very life and strength. I had no talent or pound, no gift or grace, nothing but what belonged to you." It speaks of a heart for whom God, Jesus, the gospel, and sound doctrine were not ideas flitting about in the brain but personally defining realities. "Lord, they revealed your love to me, your wisdom and power. They made your word, all of it, come alive to me as a sure and refreshing guide to understand you more fully, love you more deeply. I did not think what I was doing was worth much. Few commended me, wanted to know my life story, or thought I was very relevant, since I did not put myself forward. My soul was plagued each day by sins, my sense of insufficiency, and my troubles."

It also screams: "But loving you, Lord, I wanted to serve you. I did not always give that check or pray for that brother or cook that meal with the right spirit. I felt a tug-o-war in my heart at times: wanting and yearning to do the good yet finding much sin within me. I kept looking to your cross for forgiveness, your reign for strength, and your intercession for support and comfort. Lord, seeing now your glory, how wondrous you are, the kingdom prepared for those who love you, I see more clearly all that I should have done but left undone. I am ashamed of myself. I trust in your mercy now as I did in my earthly course. Anything good in me, you did it. Your love and cross are my only boast."

And that is exactly how Jesus will view his sheep: covered with his blood, struggling against sin yet clinging to him, doing good even while feeling in themselves much evil. He will call them his own in that hour. All they did was unto him; all they did not do is forgiven. Their hearts were upright, desiring him, willing to take the lowest seat at the feast just to be with him and learn of him – O, just to touch the hem of his robe to be healed a little more today, love a little more sincerely, serve a little more diligently.

The goats? Words, slogans, drama; self, selfishness, sounding the trumpet as they pray and work, even if they did wondrous things (Matt. 7:21-23). It was not "unto me," not prompted by sincere love to the King, his own life and Spirit in us. It was lawless, disobedient, and self-promoting. It did not build upon the word of the King. Let us labor to know more of this "unto me," to know and love the Lord Jesus, and devote our lives to him in faith, humility, and obedience. Know him personally, savingly, powerfully. He is all our life and hope, joy and peace. Serve him diligently, humbly, adoringly. He will soon say, "You did it unto me."

Twelve Baskets

Having compassion upon the hungry multitudes, our Lord took five small loaves and two fishes, just a little food carried by a boy in his pouch, gave thanks, and multiplied little into abundance. What love and power united to feed the hungry that day! Since he can do this, we should never doubt his ability and willingness to provide for us. He loves to give his people a feast, to provide beyond all expectation. Each day he does this in so many ways that we are usually stupefied before his goodness and miserably fail to thank him. We focus upon what we think we lack rather than upon what he has already placed into our hands.

After feeding these thousands, our Lord instructed the disciples to "gather up the fragments that remain, that nothing be lost" (John 6:12). His command is worthy of our careful consideration, for in the blinding glory of the feeding itself, it is easy to pass over this seemingly insignificant detail. Twelve baskets held the fragments from the feast. There was far more food left over than they had in the beginning! There was a basket for each disciple. Were they not to learn from this that the Lord possessed sufficient resources to provide for them?

Whether in a dark dungeon for the gospel or hated by all men or feeling oppressed beyond all possibility of recovery, our Lord has fullness of grace and strength. His disciples were never to forget those baskets. We grow fearful when we forget them. No matter how great a legitimate need may be, there stands the living Bread, ready to share of his fullness with us. He takes care of every bird. He clothes the flowers with luxuriant blossoms. Everything eats from his hand. Therefore, our Savior said, "Take no thought for tomorrow" (Matt. 6:34). He who owns the cattle on a thousand hills will never fail to take care of his children. He feeds his enemies. His friends should never doubt his faithfulness.

But there is something more here. Grace is never to be wasted. Our Lord wanted the multitudes to see more in this feeding than the bread (John 6:26). He wanted them to see beyond the provision of earthly bread to the true manna from heaven, his divine power, grace, and love. He wanted them to understand his sufficiency, that they need look for nothing but what they find in him. Think of all the ways the Lord has abundantly provided for us in the past. Do we remember what he gave us? Do we thank him for it? Whether he chooses to give us abundance or just enough, it was undeserved. His gifts to sinners are always gracious, always part of those promises which are "yes" in him (2 Cor. 1:20). Our ingratitude to God is not the least of our sins. It blocks joy. It blinds us to the baskets the Lord has already filled, which are a testimony to what he will yet do.

Thus, when God fills our baskets with his grace, he expects us to store it up. His faithfulness must be remembered (Ps. 119:52,55). Has he forgiven our sins? Never must the memory of our Savior's precious blood or the glory of his sufferings grow cold. Did he help us in our hour of need? One deliverance should lead us to praise and serve him forever with joyful hearts. But he has delivered us countless times. He has comforted us so many times that his faithfulness should never be questioned but anticipated. He has filled the basket of a believing memory with far greater blessings than bread and fish. He has given us himself. Treasure his blessings, child of God. Never forget them. If necessary, and it likely will be, keep a diary of every answered prayer, unexpected provision, and joyous feast.

We shall need these records. There will be more seasons in the desert. We need to remember the Lord's power and faithfulness so that in leaner times, we are able to feast upon his past goodness and depend upon him. Think of when he first brought you to saving faith in his Son. You came to Jesus only because the Father drew you (John 6:37,44). He could have left you starving in the wilderness of sin, and you could not have complained of any injustice. He brought you out. He split asunder the Rock of Ages, our Lord Jesus, on the cross, and poured forth rivers of grace. Have you forgotten? Has worldliness or fear or frustration emptied your basket of gratitude? Unless we keep in constant memory the wonders of God's salvation, the deceitfulness of riches and worldly lusts will choke out God's word (Mark 4:19). It happened to these very men whom the Lord fed.

When difficult times come or we hear hard doctrines that make us uncomfortable, our first thought is to complain and fret. Perhaps you heard a sermon that really stepped on your toes. You may be having trouble with your spouse or children. Perhaps your present employment seems precarious, and you feel sure you are about to be let go or have your wages diminished. You then look around at the city of man, with all its absurdities masquerading as things of importance. You hear its politicians stirring up strife and class envy, robbing and scheming, lying and killing. Sin's blindness and ignorance are truly terrifying. You wonder whether your children will be safe; whether you will be safe.

Remember those baskets. God has preserved his people through some very bleak hours, trials of such magnitude that it seemed as if God's Church would not survive. The memory of God's goodness saw them through those hours, and we are their children. What will pass on to our children? That we made a good living and enjoyed our retirement years? That our house was always clean and our clothing fashionable? We set so much importance upon the meat that perishes (John 6:27).

It is far better to pass on the memory of the way the Lord delivered you from the dominion of your sins, led you to a place where you could hear his word preached, or encouraged you to persevere in the faith when you were so ferociously assailed by doubt that only God's power upheld you. Perhaps that diary of God's faithfulness would be used to kindle another reformation in the heart of one of your children – if you had only kept it, spoken of his goodness, thanked rather than complained. And assuming you are growing in love for the Savior, is not he the bread that does not perish (John 6:27)? Has he not satisfied you when in the world's eyes, you were barely making it?

He is the true bread (John 6:35). This is what the feeding is supposed to teach us. Whatever our need, Jesus Christ is our life and fullness. Whatever our temptations, he is powerful to overcome them. However pressed we are with responsibility, he has sufficient strength to keep us on the path of faithfulness. This is what those men were supposed to think after eating those bread and fishes. Let us run to Jesus Christ. This was a fine repast, but

170

we want him – not to be our political deliverer, for from all such delusions, he withdraws himself (John 6:15). He is a King, the only rightful King of men and nations (Rev. 1:5), but he will reign not by human might and expectations but by feeding men with himself. Unless we are eating him – believing him, desiring him, loving and obeying him – we have no life in us (John 6:53).

And this life is abundant (John 10:10); he is abundant. There were leftovers. Think of what this means. You feel tempted to a particular sin. The pull of the flesh is strong. Stop and remember how the Lord has saved you and offers himself to you. Call upon him and abide in his word, and he will strengthen you with the living, eternal bread to resist sin and continue yielding yourself to God. Remember how he helped you in the past to overcome sin, or particularly encouraged you with a sermon, or wonderfully refreshed you through prayer, perhaps that very morning. Will we throw away his abundance for a little fleeting pleasure? He fills our basket. What love and compassion he continues to pour out upon us! All the good he has done us, all the tears we have cried due to our stupidity and fears that he has collected into his bottle, he has done these things for us because he loves us. He loves to share his fullness with us. Having fed us once, he will never stop feeding us.

We must labor for this bread (John 6:27). We shall have to trust him to provide for us. Trust is hard work, as anyone who has done any real trusting will tell you. To continue believing that God will provide when we do not see how he can, or to resist sin when you simply want to give in and end the pressure, these are choice morsels for which we must labor. I fear this is where too many of us fail. We profess to believe this, but when our Lord presses us a little, delays in answering our prayers, and tests our faith, we grow weary.

He will feed us, for he has promised. But we cannot go to sleep and simply expect him to drop the bread into our lap. He expects us to stir ourselves up to ask, seek, and knock. He expects us to carry the basket of his grace with us, the living memory of his power and faithfulness already shown to us. Waste nothing, child of God, however small the fragments may seem. His grace today is

Twelve Baskets

the food that will sustain you tomorrow as you journey onward to
God's eternal city.

Hard Words

Having an infant in our home again is quite a joy. I have not laughed so much in years and had forgotten the simple pleasure of stacking up blocks and knocking them over. I am also relearning a firm "no." Watching his response to this little word is a combination of comedy and tragedy. It is as if his small world comes to a screeching halt – the quivering lip, a few tears, and sometimes a howl. He inherited this from me. His daddy has no great love for the hard words and warnings that disrupt my tenacious God-delusion. Only by crying as a little child and looking to my Father to overcome my willfulness and pride can I expect him to help me. He resists the proud. I need to become that child of which our Savior spoke.

Life is filled with hard words from our Father. Some of the doctrines of Scripture are impossible to fathom and challenging to accept, especially those that reveal him to be a God of such absolute sovereignty that our only hope is his sovereign mercy. We are not in control. We cannot move him to do what he does not want to do, what he knows is not in our best interest, what will not reveal his glory and our need of him every moment. His "no's" are so wise and holy. Still, we writhe and cry when we hear them. Like little ones, we want everything to be "yes" – life on our terms with as little difficulty as possible.

Some of the hardest words our Lord ever spoke are found in John 6. The day before he taught them to the multitude gathering in Capernaum, he had fed them all with five loaves of bread and a few fishes. Life was grand that day. Jesus Christ revealed his power and compassion. There were even leftovers, which he instructed his disciples to gather up, so that "nothing be lost" (v. 12). This was a Savior the Jews could embrace. Some of them wanted to take him by force and immediately set him up as a king (v. 15) – a kingdom of plenty, a veritable utopia, without work, money, or faith, just bread and meat, and lots of it. These sorts of expectations are very familiar to us today. Men love this perversion of the kingdom of God, except now they substitute the printing press, government paternity, and equality by theft.

The morning came. Jesus and his disciple had passed over the Sea of Galilee. The crowds were hungry again, so they came searching for Jesus. He understood them perfectly. They followed him because they wanted more bread (v. 26). He urged them to "labor for the meat that does not perish," the bread that gives eternal life (v. 27). To have this bread, they must believe on him (v. 29). Instead, they asked for more signs, more proof; yesterday's miracle was insufficient (v. 30). They want him to do what Moses did for them: feed them for forty years with bread from heaven (v. 31). He offered himself as the true bread who came down from heaven to give life to the world (v. 33).

They were interested; they wanted this bread (v. 34). It sounded better than what Moses gave. Then, Jesus proclaimed: "I am the bread of life: he that cometh to me shall never hunger; and he that believeth on me shall never thirst" (v. 35). But they cannot have this bread unless the Father gives them faith to come to him and receive it (v. 37). This is not bread that they control and define. It is out of their reach unless God sovereignly and mercifully gives them faith to believe and eat.

This is too much for them. His words were wondrously clear, but they were coming from him. We know this man; how can he say, "I am the bread which came down from heaven" (v. 41)? Jesus now pressed them to the breaking point. Many preachers would have found a way to lower the bar and win the crowd: not the bread, but a bread; you have the strength to stretch out your hand and take it; you can eat and still hold on to your favorite things, for God wants you to be happy. Jesus played no such games with divine truth.

You cannot come to me unless the Father draws you, drags you by an internal renewal that is wholly beyond your ability (v. 44). If you know the Father, he will teach you of me, and you will come to me (v. 45). Do not try and figure this out by your reason or experience; I am the only one who has seen the Father (v. 46). I alone can reveal him; apart from me, all is darkness. Again: I am the bread of life (v. 48). Your fathers ate manna and died; if you eat me, you will live forever (vv. 49-50). You are dead; I must give my flesh if you are to have life (v. 51).

A fight practically broke out among the crowd (v. 52). Jesus added fuel to the fire. Unless you eat me, you have no life in you (v. 53). If you eat me, you will live forever, and I will raise you up (v. 54). My flesh is the only meat; my blood is the only drink (v. 55). I dwell only with those who eat me: take me into their inmost being by faith, live only by me, want nothing but me (v. 56). The living Father has sent me, and the only living men are those who eat me (v. 57). The crowd is dumbfounded. Never did mortal men hear such words! They were offended at our Savior's absolute claim of personal sufficiency and exposure of their emptiness (v. 61). To have this bread meant admitting a hunger deeper than the stomach: void of any righteousness, strength, or hope save that which this man gives.

Even his broader group of disciples murmured at his words. Jesus now pressed his claims with an alarming clarity. What if you see me ascend up where I was before (v. 62)? What divine, confident eternity, authority, and sovereignty flow from his blessed lips! Then, Jesus proclaimed aloud the thought that haunted them, the conclusion they wished to avoid at all costs. "The flesh profits nothing." You cannot understand or possess this bread on your terms. Only the Spirit, my Spirit, gives life and enables a man to believe and eat. As for my words that you hate, "They are spirit, and they are life" (v. 63). But you cannot have this life unless the Father gives it to you (v. 65).

This was the final straw. His Galilean popularity for all practical purposes ended at this point. Most of his disciples no longer walked with him. He offered them himself. They did not want him. His words were too hard, too absolute, too unbearably humbling. Jesus turned to the twelve. "Will you also go away" (v. 67)? Ever the first to confess, Peter made one of the most glorious confessions to be found in all of Scripture. "Lord, to whom shall we go? You have the words of eternal life. And we believe and are sure that you are that Christ, the Son of the living God" (vv. 68-69).

When reason reaches its limit, there is the Christ of God speaking the words of life. When there is a struggle to make his words match our experience, we say good-bye to experience and trust the hard words of the Son of God. When he sifts us so deeply that we feel he is turning us inside out, stomping on all our pride and delusions of strength, there is the Bread of life, offering himself to us. Hard words or no, they are the words of the One sent down from heaven. He will feed us with the true bread. He will raise us up on the last day. However hard he presses upon us, we must eat of him, believe in him, come to him, cling to him. There is no one else to whom we may go. No other religion. No other philosophy. There is no one. It is either Jesus Christ or starvation in the wilderness of our pride. It is either Jesus Christ or utter emptiness now and darkness forever in hell.

These and other hard words of Jesus you must hear and believe if you would have him and obtain his everlasting kingdom. His words come with piercing power. They shatter our delusions: about God, ourselves, and the nature of life itself. We think we are strong, smart. Someone will figure out our problems. Some other solution will present itself. None is forthcoming. Bring out your best technology, political and economic systems, religions, and philosophies. All tried; all failed; all empty. There is but one bread for sin-ravished men, one source of life and salvation: Jesus Christ, the crucified Savior, the resurrected Lord of glory.

If you would eat him, expect to feel dumbfounded before his word, convicted of your sinfulness, and so challenged in your assumptions about life that he alone can come and save you. Depend upon it. This bread is too precious to be combined with the world's filthy food, too holy to leave us unchanged. Wondering, humbled, yet confident in God's mercy, confess with Peter. Become the little child who cries for one food only: the safe food of God, his Christ.

He loves us too much to leave our idols intact and our pride untouched. He tells us we have no life in us because he tells us the truth and offers himself to be the true food and drink of our souls. He gave his flesh for us on the cross; his blood has cleansed us. As hard as it may be, eat him: by faith in his saving work, trusting his word, and looking to nothing else to satisfy you. He is the living bread that has come down from heaven. Reject him, refuse to trust him when circumstances overwhelm you, refuse to believe the truth about yourself, and starve. Eat, and live. Eat and never die. Eat and live forever, feasting on the true bread.

Jesus' Fire

Recent sickness in our congregation has left many, including me, asking, "Lord, is it I?" I am "sold in sin, and in sin did my mother conceive me." Having known God's truth, I have often wandered from it. Covetous, lazy, and selfish – this unholy trinity of folly plagues my heart. While it is easier to ask, "Lord, is it he," we should remember that all but Judas asked, "Is it I?" He was the last to ask, but only after Jesus read his heart like an open book, unsettling and driving him into the dark night of treachery (Matt. 26:23-25).

Through Jesus Christ, we are invited to come boldly to the throne of grace to receive mercy and grace. We must come with praise and thankfulness, and also with pointed self-examination and confession of our sins. Have we been the praying people God calls us to be? Are we merciful people, caring for one another and the lost around us, bearing with one another's weakness, and thinking the best of one another, forgiving "seven times seventy?"

Or, have we become self-appointed censors of others, arrogant in our knowledge, self-loving and self-trusting? Have the elders been faithful in overseeing the congregation, encouraging and disciplining its members, and going after the wayward? Have we partaken of the Lord's Supper and at the same time eaten at the table of demons – worldliness, lust, idolatry, hatefulness in our hearts and homes? Are we thankful that he gives us his word? Have we prayed for the pastor and elders, submitted to their biblical counsel, and sought out their guidance? "The curse causeless shall not come" (Prov. 26:2). While it is beyond us to know the full mind of God, we know what he has revealed (Deut. 29:29). If we are unfaithful in known duties of faith, love, and doctrine, we may be certain that if he loves us, he will chasten us. His correction is never haphazard.

Though much of modern life is designed to circumvent hardship, the word of God holds true: "The Lord tries the righteous" (Ps. 11:5). Man's efforts to insulate himself from God cannot alter his government of the world and shepherding of his people. He will test and purify faith (1 Pet. 1:7). He will use whatever means he deems wise to confront our sins and form us into the image of his Son. Trials of various sorts, so far from being a cause of anxiety, should make us rejoice (James 1:2). It is a blessing to be brought low, to feel our weakness, to face our mortality and total dependence upon God. "When I am weak, then I am strong" (2 Cor. 12:10). It is a paradox of heaven-born faith. When life is going well, pride often mounts a fresh assault. As rare as Job is the man who seeks God with fervency when all is well. Trouble is usually required to wake us up so that we pray as we breathe and hunger after God's word as our daily bread.

God is wise and his providence diverse, so his refining fires do not take the same form in all. Some who never struggle financially are beset with doubts and must do hard battle before gaining assurance of salvation. Others to whom he grants fuller assurance may struggle with disease or with children. When these troubles come, we want them "fixed," but since God tests the righteous, if "fixing" means "getting rid of the trouble" then we may be fighting against the very pressures to which the Lord wants us to submit.

This life will not be heaven. We should expect to be tested and tried. There is much corruption in us, much that dishonors God and provokes his abiding, holy presence with us. It is because he loves us that he chastens and disciplines, so that we "might be partakers of his holiness" (Heb. 12:10). Only the holy are happy (Ps. 119:1; John 13:17), and God sends trouble to make us happy. He chastens to fill us with his joy and to confirm that we are truly his sons and daughters. Immediately after the voice came from heaven, "Thou are my beloved Son, in whom I am well pleased," he was "led up of the Spirit into the wilderness to be tempted of the devil" (Matt. 3:17-4:1). What was true of him is true of all God's children. He will have our sonship tested in the fire so that his power may be revealed and our faith purified.

But this will result only if we yield ourselves to him. We want his fires to be extinguished – marital strife to cease, health restored, children to be more obedient, finances to be more secure. We cry and weep when these troubles come, complain and fret, or grit our teeth and try to bear them as best we can. Are we boasting in them (2 Cor. 12:9)? We must be careful here. It is possible to have a "life is so hard" morbidity that the spirit is crushed, but this is really pride. Only God can teach us to boast or glory in our troubles. Faith believes his promises through the tears. It trusts his wisdom through the pain. It sees beyond the immediate to the goal of trouble: more love for God, less inclination toward sin, more delight in God himself.

Our Lord learned this obedience by suffering (Heb. 5:8-9). It is the only way to learn it – not "get this cross off my back" but "make this cross a blessing to me, Lord Jesus. I do not understand the reason you have brought this into my life, but I understand that you are good and faithful, wise and strong. If you want me to suffer through this, it must be for my good. I do not have to understand. I only want your strength, to bear your image more fully, and to have heavenly affections that delight in you."

The Lord's sifting work sometimes seems so severe that we seriously wonder whether or not we are on the right path at all. We question ourselves. Who am I? Is what I believe true? Am I sincere? Maybe I am a hypocrite, or in the wrong place, or need to make a change. When the Lord touches our health, family, or vocation, anxiety and fear raise their ugly heads. For some, this leads to the proverbial mid-life crisis. The Lord certainly wants us to make changes for the good. Yet, when he is sifting us, peripheral life changes may temporarily mask the deeper issues, but they do not resolve them. Feeling better about one's appearance or home or automobile is often confused with actually being a better, godlier person. We can change the outside, but God alone can truly change the inside.

It is said of our Lord that he is "like a refiner's fire" (Mal. 3:2). He baptizes with "the Holy Ghost, and with fire" (Matt. 3:11). "Fire" is a strong word for this work. It is our natural reflex to draw back from fire, but it is perilous to draw back from him. When his fires rage in our homes or work, he is teaching us that we are not in control and cannot make our children godly or our spouse better, but that we must trust him no matter how miserable we are in these areas. We look around for someone to blame. We try to change everything. We want to escape the pressure. We cry, but he does not seem to hear. We look around for saviors. Some try new pastors or churches. Women with weak husbands often migrate to church leaders who appear to have it together. Men with unsatisfying or impossible to please wives turn to other women or simply withdraw emotionally. Children who feel they cannot make their parents happy run into the arms of the first person who offers warmth and acceptance. These are self-preservation measures. They are also ways we refuse to let our Savior's fires burn – like a fever burning away the disease.

It will do no good but great harm to pull back from his heat. Peter pulled back from our Lord's frequent warning about his pride, and look where it led him – base denial. We often do the same. Strong preaching or confronting elders are rejected because the pressure feels too great. Like Rachel, we want to be in Jacob's tent but hide our household idols. This is one reason there is so much migration from church to church: never able to settle, running when the fire of his word is applied, hiding, moving to the next place, and reporting how abused I was before. This is children running to their room to pout when confronted by their sins. We do not need to pout or change our doctrine. We do not need fresh faces. We need to submit to Jesus Christ. If we must wander for forty years in the wilderness because of our sins, so be it. If we must endure a difficult spouse for our entire life, so be it. Might our spouse need to change? Yes, but his lack of change does not justify our bitterness or unfaithfulness. Rather, we must boast in our weaknesses, for Jesus knows that we need this particular marriage, children, and job so that we would learn obedience through suffering, patience, and the joy of obeying God.

To run from the fire is to run from Jesus Christ. Peter braved the wind-tossed waves to come to Jesus. As long as he kept his eyes fixed upon Jesus, he walked on water. Think of the area in your life in which the Lord is calling you to submit to him, to submit to his refining fire: a lust that needs to be decisively mortified; a fear that must be overcome; a family change in priority or practice. The match is lit. You want to pull back. The Lord has brought this fire into your life so you will learn obedience to him. He loves you. He would have you know his strength, his wisdom. He would have you cry for grace and strength. Did he not cry to his Father? Are you better than he? Can you expect a different path than the one he walked? It is only by yielding to him that peace will come: peace through righteousness (Ps. 119:165), peace like a river (Isa. 48:18; 66:12), his peace in the fire.

All I Ever Did

One of the most thought-provoking statements in the Gospels must be the Samaritan woman's excited declaration to her fellow townsmen: "Come, see a man, which told me all things that I ever did" (John 4:29). Equally compelling is her following question: "Is not this the Christ?"

I doubt seriously whether we would be excited about meeting such a man. Imagine what this means: long-forgotten words and deeds exposed, shocked and embarrassed by the unexpected reminder of secret sins. "All" includes the thoughts of the heart: the filthy sewer out of which sin slithers. In her case, it was a life of sensuality, marriages, and divorces, her discontent, worldliness, and vanity. Put your "all things" in place of hers. Would we not fear such openness to others about meeting such a man? Some of our skeletons would have to be released from the closet in order to prove such an astounding claim.

Once a hider, this woman runs into the light. She seems relieved, abounding in joy, very much willing to share with the whole world her new found freedom: from herself and from her past. Unlike her, we might very well flee from such a person: too much danger of exposure here. We like our masks, our pretending and pretense, for others to think well of us. We might occasionally reveal a few of our lesser failures, just enough to appear humble and transparent, but almost always with the added claim that this is all behind us now. We are now doing quite well. Not this woman.

She was insistent. Apparently, she went from house to house, quickly, or perhaps to the center of town activity. Her confession surprised few. Her past could not very well be hidden. Yet, whereas everyone likely knew about "this woman" – she was likely the object of many quiet sneers – now they are hearing the story from her. As an aside, is there anything like honest confession to put suspicion to silence, to put the conscience to rest? As the Proverb says, "By mercy and truth iniquity is purged" (16:6).

All I Ever Did

But she has more to relate than a sordid past; she has a person to present. She is convinced that this is the Christ. Who else can he be? He knew her inmost secrets without her breathing a word to him. In his light, her darkness was penetrated, its tyranny overthrown, its fears removed. The light was painful, at first, and she had tried to change the subject to one of the theological disputes of her age. Light forced itself upon her. This man said he would give her living, satisfying water. He answered her doctrinal question, but it was the personal probing that gripped her attention. Then, he identified himself. In response to her "I know that Messiah is coming, which is called Christ," he said, "I that speak unto you am he" (John 4:25-26). This was enough for her. She believed and was cleansed. She believed and confessed: her past, her Savior, her living water.

We must meet this man. What a surprising relief it is to do so. That he knows all we ever did means he knows us better than we know ourselves. It is not simply that we need no longer hide and pretend in his presence but that meeting him we learn who we truly are. All has not been well with us. We have been troubled, weakened, and ensnared in many sins, fears, and hurtful lusts. We licked our wounds, but they were not healed. Many excuses we make and remedies we try without obtaining relief. What others know or suspect about us is troubling, yes, but living with ourselves is far worse. There are moments conscience simply will not be satisfied by our many public masks and private delusions, when a little light creeping in throws us into utter confusion and despair. Yet, we could not find the cure and did not even understand the disease. This is who we are until we meet such a man, until he tells us all we ever did.

This man alone can save us. He knows the truth about us. He is the truth. Before him, all lies must flee. His light does not content itself with a few peripheral sins, the symptoms of deeper corruption. He goes right to the heart of our most guarded secrets and fears. The wonder of the gospel is that though Jesus Christ knows all our filth, as well as our attempts to cover it up, he still died for us. Here is love unfathomable and mercy immeasurable. Although we were sinners, Christ died for us.

Our blindness, delusion, and light-resistance could not quench his love or prevent his sacrifice. We were utterly helpless, totally depraved, and completely dead in our sins. Darkness was our home, our false friend; we loved it because our deeds were evil. Still, he would not be put off. "I must go through Samaria" (4:4); there is a woman there I must deliver. She is hated, isolated, and enslaved. She deserves to be, for her sins are many. I alone can deliver her. I must tell her all she ever did." Can we ever understand or adore the love of Jesus: that he came to our corrupt Samaria, confronted us with the truth about ourselves, and brought us out of our dark caves of self-preservation? Never.

Never also means now. In the course of our lives, we have constant need to meet this man, the God-man. Even as believers, darkness is always lurking, craving for a corner here, a closet there. Our reflex is self-preservation, perhaps not under a full mask but a partial one, not full-blown self-deceit but enough to keep up the pretense that all is well. We still crave the acceptance and praise of men, to be thought better than we are, to avoid the direct light, to hold on to self. We must meet Jesus. There can be no sincerity before God without him: no saving brokenness, no growth in holiness, no healthy conscience.

For this reason, David prayed: "Search me, O God, and know my heart, and see if there be any wicked way in me" (Ps. 139:23). It is as if he cried: "Lord, I still feel my corruption, bubbling within. I still cannot know myself unless your light comes to me. I want you to tell me my sins, even the secret ones that I have hidden from myself." Here is a remarkable thing about the redeemed. Though the whole world hides from the light of God's holiness, believers want it. We are unsettled by his dazzling, penetrating brightness, to be sure, made more than a little uncomfortable, forced to cry out for mercy.

But here is our only safety, the only way we are prevented from returning to masks and hiding: when God's holiness and total knowledge of us does not scare us away from him but draws us closer. In Jesus' light, the heart is no longer terrorized by fear of hell's terrors but flooded with desire for heaven's fellowship. I

185

need light, the lover of God's holiness confesses. I need to be told all I ever did and what I am doing that displeases my Savior.

This is the fountain of that sincerity apart from which there is no saving faith or health. Hypocrites put on the appearance of religion. They give up a few side sins to hold on to more cherished ones. For them, godliness is all about avoiding the full light of truth and of keeping the respect and approval of men above all else. It is doing outward good while still in the chains of inward corruption. The hypocrite does not want to be told all he ever did, and he certainly does not want others to know it. He repents like Pharaoh: when the heat gets too great, temporarily, partially, from a desire to preserve his position, his self-delusion; or like Judas: when it is too late, without any hope of mercy, out of personal despair, when his lies are finally exposed. The weight of his guilt does not lead to the Christ but to the devil, to the end of a rope. When the hypocrite reaches this place, he would rather end it all than face his true self. He is too bitter that the delusion had to end. He loves himself more than mercy, God, and truth.

Sincere hearts and full assurance of faith are the dearly purchased blessings of the gospel. Our need for them is great at all times: for open, honest, sin-confessing and sin-forsaking churches and homes, in a culture that has a mask of self-deception tightly welded to it, with too much noise to face the truth. Let us scatter the secrecy by running through our communities and towns, making the confession of the Samaritan woman and bringing men to hear Jesus. We must hear from him daily what we have done and be taught by him who we truly are. There is no despair here, and no need to fear. When he tells us the truth, it is because he loves us and intends to save us. He brings us into the light of God's holiness. O, the refreshment, the liberty, and the hope that comes to us before the throne of God, standing there without hiding, having our self-deception burned up in the light of his holiness, having him speak peace and mercy to our hearts! There our Savior is: our faithful Advocate, honest Friend, powerful Savior.

When we come before the Lord Jesus and hears the truth about ourselves, we shall hide from our sins no longer. We shall hide our sinfulness no longer. Liberation and light will open our mouths to confess: come meet this Man, this Christ. Throw off your grave clothes; put away yours masks. Come to holiness, to light, and to hope. Come to Jesus. He will tell you all you ever did.

The Good Wine

Our Savior's love for us and his surpassing loveliness are the fountain of true and abiding joy. Yet because our faith is so weak, he seems far away, glorious and desirable but remote and untouchable. Oh well, we say to ourselves, he is in heaven, surrounded by all the glittering hosts, while I am still on earth, where there is so much trouble and confusion. What good does his loveliness do me? We can hear a thousand sermons telling us that our Lord walks with us as we abide in his word, but we think such a promise is not for us. Then, losing hope, we choose bad solutions to life's problems, fall into despair, and make excuses for the dissatisfaction and bitterness we feel. Unchecked, we eventually lose our taste for God's word, which only deepens the pit of our sadness.

This is the reason we must pay the closer attention to those instances in the Gospels that reveal our Savior's overflowing heart of love and goodwill to us. Yes, he is now crowned with glory and honor. He rules the world by his power. Still, he is near to us, ever ready and able to do us good, and always open to our cries. The accounts of his love and generosity in the Gospels are designed to teach us this. Indeed, they are the divine promise that he is always with us in the ways he was with his people of old.

He does not seem to work with such glory and power now as he did then, but this is unbelief talking. We must not force him into the box of our earthly, selfish expectations. He promised to do mightier works from the right hand of his Father through the indwelling presence of his Spirit (John 14:12). Faith must rest upon his promise. If we would but seek and believe him, we would see more of his hand in our daily lives, more than enough of his love and nearness to give us comfort along our earthly pilgrimage and testify to his love.

Consider the first recorded miracle in John's gospel: the turning of water into wine (John 2:1-11). Here is a young couple on the most important day of their lives. They have run out of wine. There is whispering among the servants. The young couple is about to be embarrassed; their marriage celebration is turning into a fiasco. Though Jesus resists his mother's attempts to direct his messianic course (v. 3), he came to the wedding to manifest his glory.

Seeing six stone pots sitting nearby, he instructs the servants to fill them with water, draw out the water, and carry it into the party. Unaware of what has happened, the governor of the feast, the one who presided to make sure that all went according to custom and the guests were well-served, testified that it was far better wine than that served first – a highly unusual practice and clear evidence that they were not drinking grape juice!

The most important aspect of this miracle is its fulfillment of the Old Testament prophecies relating abundance of wine to the coming of the Messiah. Isaiah very enthusiastically compares the gospel and "sure mercies of David," our Lord Jesus Christ, with wine (55:1). Speaking of Messiah's day, Joel says that the "mountains shall drop down new wine" (3:18). Immediately after promising the rebuilding of David's tabernacle, which James declares was fulfilled in the work of Jesus Christ (Acts 15:15-17), Amos makes the same declaration as Joel (9:11-13). When the King comes to us, lowly and riding upon a foal, Zechariah prophesies his days will be known by abundance of wine (9:9,17). We might say that by this miracle, Jesus says of himself: "I am the wine of the world; I am the delight of life."

Wine is one of God's choice gifts. It makes man's heart glad and is a fitting symbol of the blessed days of the new covenant. That our Lord chose as one of his first miracles the turning of water into wine shows that he is the choicest gift of God. He makes our heart glad. Whatever crosses we carry and long-standing sins against which we must fight, Jesus is the wine of life. To know him is to have joy while suffering. Do we have this joy, or do we walk around with heavy hearts and sad faces? Perhaps we have not drunk enough wine, enough of Jesus. He is the same yesterday and today. He still satisfies, offers his joy to us as our comfort in this world, and pledges to give us joy as we walk with him in obedience (John 15:9-11).

Struggling believer, take your eyes off yourself, off your problems, off the world in its rebellion – look into the face of Jesus

Christ, believe his word, cast your cares upon him, and be refreshed from his fullness. But you must believe and come to him as he revealed himself in his word. Before you taste of his joy, expect to be sifted, to have your sins confronted, even to be tested. Will you keep coming if you are not refreshed immediately? Do you want to feel better, or do you want Jesus Christ himself, regardless of how you feel?

He will not turn you away, for he is incomparably generous. What a gift he made to the young couple, who were too poor to provide enough wine for their wedding feast! Each of the water pots contained between eighteen and twenty-seven gallons; multiplied times six, that is over one hundred gallons of the best wine anyone ever tasted! Long after the wedding day ended, this couple would enjoy this wondrous wine. Economically and socially, our Lord elevated them that day. The glory he revealed by this miracle is this: there is fullness of joy and grace in him, abundant, never-ending, personally satisfying and life-transforming. He is the best wine, and we cannot exhaust his fullness.

We do not taste more of his fullness because our expectations of him are too low. We are too little acquainted with him. We push away his cheering, strengthening presence by our sins and fears. We forget that he is our righteousness, anchor, refuge, and peace. Through faith in him, we are invited to drink from the rivers of pleasure, God's own presence, settled love, and rejoicing in us. Jesus is not stingy with his joy; we are stingy in our views of him! Tolerating such low and unworthy thoughts, we rob ourselves of the new wine that is still flowing down from the mountains of God's holiness, an ever-broadening river of delight (Ezek. 47:1-5).

The enjoyment of wine requires training one's palate. The soul also has a palate. Feed it upon the world's poison wine and rotten food, and you will not have the right taste for the Lord Jesus. The only way to train our taste buds to delight in him is to stay away from the bad wine and go right for the best. Begin each day seeking the Lord. You may be a babe in Christ, unable to take much solid food yet, but only milk. Still, nurse at our Savior's breast by coming to his sacred truth, asking him to give you his

Spirit as your teacher, and begin taking in the sweet wine of his promises. You will mature. You cannot sincerely seek Jesus Christ and not grow in grace and in the knowledge of him (2 Pet. 1:8).

Drink the wine of the Gospels constantly. Memorize and meditate upon our Savior's abundance revealed in them so you can recall his fullness and generosity when you grow thirsty as you battle against sin. As you drink him, your faith will increase. Soon, you will read the Scriptures as living memorials of his abundance and pledges of his presence. You will be surprised by the joy he gives, as this couple was by the wine. Our Lord is full of such unexpected blessings. When we come honestly to him, by his Spirit he gives confirmation of his presence and power sustaining you. This may be strength to prevail over a sudden temptation. In other seasons, he gives joyful patience in adversity, earthly provision when you did not expect it, hope in his promises, and greater constancy in affection for him. The wine of his love for you is inexhaustible and, like a good wine, complex, various in its tastes and hues, never dull, bitter, or flat. His love and loveliness will carry you to heaven. It will give you joy on earth.

We need the wine of our Savior's love, for we do not yet drink it anew with him in his Father's kingdom. In our resurrection bodies, surrounded by the whole shining company of his saints and angels, to the everlasting joy of our souls, we shall drink with him. We shall drink him – forever, in fullness of joy and abundance of life we cannot now conceive, with peace, love, and joy growing throughout eternity. Keep this promised moment before you, for we have trials to face, enemies to overcome, and sorrows to carry. Many nations around us are burning under God's wrath and the misery of those who refuse to come to the wedding feast. We are caught up in these events, in our Savior's dashing to pieces the water pots of human vanity. The stench of fear and unbelief and compromise is growing. Only one thing will drive it away: the joy of new wine, the joy of Jesus Christ.

Drinking of him often, we shall speak of him more, terrify God's enemies by loving, forgiving, and praying for them, and find, perhaps, our own family, those who know you best, surprised by the change in us. It is because we have tasted the new wine.

191

Already we see the wedding feast set, Jesus Christ inviting us, standing at the finish line of faith's race, cheering us on, sustaining us, giving us enough sips of his loveliness and generosity to help us overcome the world. Let us pass by all other cups and drink only him.

~6~

Walking with Glory

Bearing the Cross

The heart of Christian discipleship is cross-bearing. Cross-bearing is not stoic acceptance of the creaks and pains of advancing age. It is not bearing the morning drive or going without because the credit cards are maxed. Such things, great and small, are the common lot of fallen humanity. Trivialization of cross-bearing exerts a depressing influence upon the soul of every true disciple. Something far more pointed and glorious is intended by our Savior's frequent declarations about bearing the cross.

In his most notable teaching on cross-bearing, the Gospels indicate that it followed Peter's rejection of Jesus' announcement of his pending death (Matt. 16:22-24; Mark 8:31-35; Luke 9:20-24). It is evident that Peter thought such a shameful death beneath the dignity of the Savior, whom he had just confessed as "the Christ, the Son of the living God." In response, Jesus not only rebuked Peter as siding with Satan, which may be a backward reference to Satan's temptation to Jesus to seize the crown without bearing the cross, but he also pressed the duty of cross-bearing upon all his disciples. Without cross-bearing, we cannot be his disciples.

It would appear, then, that cross-bearing is directly related to the humiliation of Christ, his rejection by the world, and his death on the shameful and cursed cross. Applied personally, to bear the cross is to shoulder the shame of our Savior's death, embrace God's war against sin and rebellion, and resist the temptation to seek the easy path. Ours is not a vicarious or propitiatory cross-bearing. Our cross-bearing is following our Savior zealously in his resistance to the world, the flesh, and the devil, making his cross our only boast, and testifying to the world the necessity of faith in a crucified Savior in order to be reconciled to God and escape the wrath to come.

Cross-bearing presses deeply upon a sinful trait of fallen man. Not only do we, like Peter, prefer to receive the crown without bearing the cross, but we also desire to have salvation on our own terms, with as little personal sacrifice as possible. When the rich young ruler came to Jesus, he claimed to have kept the law perfectly (Mark 10:20). In one word, Jesus exposed the idol of his shallow heart: his possessions. You lack one thing, Jesus told him. Sell all you have, give to the poor, take up the cross, and follow me. Get rid of your idol. The man went away sad, for he had great possessions. Our Savior did not mean that wealth is necessarily opposed to cross-bearing, though wealth does pose great temptation to those who possess it. Cross-bearing is opposed to self-sufficiency, selfishness, and love of this world. This passage emphasizes a fundamental feature of cross-bearing. There can be no salvation without it, for cross-bearing is essentially a renunciation of the world's pleasures and sins in single-hearted, exclusive devotion to Jesus Christ.

By his entire life our Savior demonstrated the meaning of cross-bearing. His life was the most compelling example of self-denial in the history of the world – a willing renunciation of his rightful claims as the eternal Son of God (Phil. 2:5-8). His lowly birth, life of poverty and suffering, and constant conflict with sin and Satan all indicate the nature of cross-bearing. He would not listen for a moment to Satan's allurement: the crown without the cross. He rejected the arrogance of his disciples, who parceled out kingdom positions without understanding the humiliation of the cross and the true meaning of discipleship. He fraternized with the sick and afflicted, the maligned and ignored, the religious outcasts – from them he could gain no earthly honor but ever sought only their repentance and restoration to God. He rode into Jerusalem on the back of a donkey – some entrance for the King of glory! And his cross – upon this horrid wooden stake he embraced and suffered the deepest shame. He removed the curse hanging over us for our sins only by becoming the curse.

Each of these ideas is inseparable from cross-bearing. It is a life of Christ-imitating self-denial, sin-resistance, and consecration to the will of the Father. It is a gospel focused-life that commits and empowers us to endure the reproach of the world and fight against sin and the flesh, all the while rejoicing in the privilege of suffering shame for his name. It is a joyful life, for herein alone do we experience the power of our Savior's death and resurrection. We bear about in our bodies the death of our Savior so that his life may also be manifested in us (2 Cor. 4:10). His cross is the tree of life; only under its shadow may we again know the life of God in the soul. It is a life that disdains the accolades of the world and the approval of men. It seeks no earthly pomp, idyllic ease, or sacrifice-less faith. Cross-bearing is the life of the disciple of Christ because it is the life of the emptied Christ manifested in those who know and adore him. He became poor for our sake to make us rich in him; we enjoy riches in him though we are poor in the eyes of the world.

For the first three centuries after our Savior's ascension, cross-bearing was the only life the church knew. She endured the hatred and reproach of the world. By bearing the cross, a growing company of unnamed, largely unheralded, and often despised disciples overcame the malice of men and ferocity of Satan. Dramatic, gospel irony was daily played out in her life, even while she fought against sin within and enemies without. By bearing the cross, she gained the crown. But then the cross was lifted. At the Council of Nicea in 325 A.D., the Roman emperor Constantine was visibly moved as the entering presbyters paraded the marks of the cross before his pompous eyes. Powerfully confronting him were disciples of Christ with missing eyes and limbs, the result of recent persecutions. Many of these men bore upon their bodies the marks of Jesus Christ, the sufferings of his cross. Constantine resolved to change permanently the fortunes of the church.

We have tended toward cross-aversion ever since. Historians are divided in their assessment of Constantine's motives and personal faith, but by his elevation of the church in terms of worldly prestige, a dangerous precedent was set. The church would no longer face the world as cross-bearers but with dignity comparable to and even surpassing that of earthly powers. The many gains and victories of the gospel would be tainted by a growing aversion to suffering for Christ's sake. Worldly dominance was sought by the leaders of the church. A form of godliness – buildings, miters, claims of succession – were chosen over the power of godliness. External, often forced unity was sought at the expense of the Spirit's unity in truth and love. The cross became a faint memory buried under ceremony and luxury.

The return to cross-bearing required the Reformation, during which a revival of the life of Jesus Christ in his Church, and with it willingness to bear his suffering and shame, obtained victory over the chains of Romanism. The world again witnessed the cost of discipleship, the price of truth, and the power of the cross.

The fires kindled by the Reformation are dying out. The dark evidence of this is a general unwillingness to bear the cross. In the West, many of us are again wedded to political agendas, economic prosperity, and a convenient faith. Like the disciples, we are parceling out kingdom honors, i.e., organizational positions, prized pulpits, political power, and economic resources, rather than bearing the cross. We increasingly rely upon political leaders to enforce our moral agenda. Our literature, how-to seminars, and preferred leaders do not drip with the blood of suffering. Instead of splinters and self-denial, we have embraced the slick and sophisticated, the easy solution, the hope of the crown without the cross. And the darkness grows: militant atheism in Europe and strident secularism in the United States. Sadly, their rebellion toward God and hatred of his word is fueled not so much by earnest believers who boast in the cross alone, love one another, and humbly seek the honor of the Savior but by hypocritical religious salesmen or self-anointed leaders of spiritual personality cults.

Cross-bearing is poised to make a comeback. We face an enemy that cannot be out-marketed, out-talked, or out-legislated. Secularism aims at nothing less than the eradication of biblical religion. It will gladly tolerate Islam before it will bow the knee to Jesus Christ; the secularists would rather bow to Allah than kiss the Son. This means that pseudo-Christianity will prove itself unable to stem the rapidly rising tide of lawlessness. Rock bands, skits, and "youth-group for adults" are impotent to resist this enemy. The people of God will be forced to make a decision. Will we embrace compromise in order to survive, or will we take up the cross? Will the Chief Shepherd mercifully wake us up in time to shoulder his gospel, its reproach and shame, its divinely appointed power to demolish strongholds? Will Christians cease depending upon political candidates, a bottom-of-the-ninth save, and "seven steps to save the world?" Or, will we return to Calvary, to the old rugged cross? If we will, the enthroned Savior will again drive his cross into the skull of Satan, crushing him under our feet. But it will be costly.

Cross-bearing means that we must not confuse being a Christian with being an American, or a capitalist, or a devotee of Constitutionalism. It means that the primary battle is not in Washington D.C. or Hollywood. It is in your life and my life, in our next door neighbor's life. Will we trust that the Lord of hosts will do what he has promised, build the kingdom of his Son upon the backs of humble disciples of Jesus Christ, who love his gospel, are unmoved by the reproach of the world, and boldly speak the truth in love? It is interesting that we have no record of an apostolic planning session: "Let's resist this particular legislative action." "Let's dress up a Mr. Gladiator who will use the Bible for a sword." They had one strategy: go into the world and proclaim the gospel to every creature under heaven. Endure hardship as a good soldier of Jesus Christ. Trust the word as God's power unto salvation.

Let us shoulder this cross again. It is far harder than any strategy being suggested today. It requires personal vigilance, consistent fellowship with Jesus Christ in the word and prayer, fellowship with the saints, and a mind transformed by the word. Live under the shadow and power of the cross, and God will bring the opportunities to stand for him – with people you see every day, by a life that shines with good works produced by the sanctifying Spirit. And have no fellowship with the unfruitful deeds of darkness – expose them. If you are too cozy with the world, your back will grow too soft for cross-bearing. Let us pray that the crucified and resurrected Savior will count us worthy by his grace to carry his cross. It has lost none of its relevance to the same old problems of sinners and none of its power to cleanse. It is still razor sharp. It will crush Satan under our feet.

A Personal Relationship with Jesus Christ

Growing up, I often heard the phrase "a personal relationship with Jesus Christ." It seemed somewhat overused, but the import was clear. Jesus Christ is a real person. To be a Christian consists of more than having a set of doctrines or practices that connect one to him outwardly, formally. There is in every true Christian a personal connection to Jesus Christ, a living union with him. Now a little older, I feel this phrase needs some modification. It needs to be made, if possible, even more personal.

Consider the way our Lord spoke in the upper room to his disciples. On that dark night that would forever define the history of our race, he described his relationship to us in such terms that even "personal" does not exhausts its depths. In John 15:9, he says that his love for us finds its parallel in his love for the Father. How does the Father love his Son? Eternally, directly, person to person, unchangeably fixed, with one will between them, and with mutual joy and delight.

More and better descriptions are undoubtedly available, but these capture the essence of the unsearchable love of God for his Beloved. And the Son loves us in this way? It boggles the mind. With all our faults and failures, fickleness and immaturity? Yes. The eleven sitting there had all these imperfections in abundance, yet, "So have I loved you." His love for sinners is an ocean whose depths cannot be measured. It is a personal love, a to-the-cross love, a love that led him to endure the wrath of God for their sake.

Then, he commands them to "continue in my love." "Continue" is the same word he has earlier used and is famously translated "abide" in me (v. 4). Keep loving me, he says. Continue learning of my love for you. This hardly seemed a night for Man of Sorrows to be talking about love. Swords would seem a more relevant theme, and a reference to the need for protection is not omitted (Luke 22:36). Preeminently, however, our Savior wanted to talk about a triad of love – the Father's love for him, his love for us, and our abiding in his love.

He tells us what continuing in his love means. "Love" is subject to much confusion. Is it a feeling? Can each man define it as he wishes? Continuing in his love is keeping his commandments (John 15:10). What? Obedience is love? Love must be very different from what men often think it is. Obedience must also be different. Obedience is the uniting of hearts and wills in holy purpose and affection. When it comes to a relationship with Jesus Christ, love is not in the eye of the beholder. He defines it. The disciple's love for his Master is always like his love for the Father: marked by obedience – sincere, zealous, sacrificing "not my will but thine" commitment.

Obedience, like love, is also personal. Obedience is more than conformity to an external code. It is guided by God's law, but the lover of Jesus does not think of himself as conforming to a standard as much as holding fast to a person – Jesus Christ. My Lord has told me of what loving him consists. He has given me his word. I love him. I want to please him. He is more real to me than my next breath. I will obey, as he obeyed the Father, whatever the cost. Thy will be done. This does not do away with the law; it makes obedience to his law intensely personal.

Then, to make this dynamic of love and obedience even more personal, he affirms that he has said these things to them so that "his joy might remain in you." Love and obedience are unto joy, as the Old Testament constantly taught (Ex. 20:6; Deut. 11:1,22; 30:20; Ps. 1:1; 119:1), but his joy? Clearly, each disciple is blessed with a joy that is objective, defined, independent of personal likes and dislikes. It is specifically Jesus' joy. What was his joy? The joy of walking in fellowship with his Father and always setting the Father before him, in whose presence is fullness of joy and life forevermore (Psalm 16:11). More concretely, Jesus' joy was the joy of obedience.

If we are to enter this circle of love, we must seek to recover a biblical view of obedience. For many, the very word brings a cringe. "Uh-oh, the preacher is talking about obedience again. He is trying to bring us under the law. Let us hear more about grace." Yet, there is no grace without obedience: not grace to be earned but grace to be enjoyed. Obedience is the fruit of grace, "for we are

A Personal Relationship with Jesus Christ

his workmanship, created in Christ Jesus unto good works, which God hath before ordained that we should walk in them" (Eph. 2:10). There is no personal relationship with Jesus Christ unless there is obedience to him. Obedience is the holy seal of his heart and life formed in us by the Spirit, so that his delight to obey his Father becomes our delight.

It is too true of us that when we think about obeying, we often wait for lightning to strike. Yes, I need to obey God, we say with a sigh, but I will wait until my circumstances change, or my wife does what she is supposed to do, or I have more money. Not obeying, we are not joyful. We wonder why. It must be the preacher's fault, or my spouse's, or my children's. We should not wonder. Jesus Christ has told us the way to joy. It is the path of loving, committed obedience. It is the path he walked, all the way to the cross, for the joy set before him, a path requiring his absolute obedience. Very often, if not always, when we determine to obey God, we suddenly find peace restored to our soul. Yes, obeying him can be extremely difficult – remember our Savior's struggle in the Garden. But it remains the path to joy and a richer experience of Jesus' love in us.

Consider those areas in your life about which you need to follow the example of David: "I thought on my ways, and turned my feet unto thy testimonies. I made haste, delayed not to keep thy commandments" (Ps. 119:59-60). Every area of disobedience is a pit of sorrow. The whole world of unbelieving men is wallowing in this pit and screaming, "NO! I will not obey God! Joy is not found in the old paths but in doing it my way. Try this. Do this. Change this." Better to follow Jesus. Let us obey God. Let us not wait to obey him or make curious excuses for disobedience like: "Well, I cannot obey until he gives me grace. I am not obeying; therefore, he must not be giving me grace. It is not my fault." Yes, it is. He gives grace in the way of obedience, as well as joy and love.

Not one of us can comprehend the incomparable joy of obeying God – not yet. It has nothing to do with trying to earn anything or looking good in the eyes of men or manipulating God to get what we want. Joyful obedience to God is the response of the believing heart to mercies already received. This was the way

202

Israel was to receive the Ten Commandments, not as a "do this to earn my favor," as if the Ten Commandments were nothing but a covenant of works republished, but as a "thank you for delivering us from Egypt" (Ex. 20:1-2). Thank you for your mercy and faithfulness; we shall gladly obey you because you have redeemed us. True obedience is joy-producing as nothing else is, for it brings the smile of God upon us. His word is eternal, fixed in the heavens (Ps. 119:89). Nothing pleases him or us more than when we can confess, "My soul hath kept thy testimonies; and I love them exceedingly" (Ps. 119:167). This was the heart of our Savior, and none was as joyful as he. His joy was so great that it led him willingly to the cross, in obedience to his Father's will.

He promises that this joy of his will remain in us as we walk in obedience as he did. This joy is the personal fruit of obedience, for he adds: "that your joy may be full." The circle of love, obedience, and joy, the Father, Jesus Christ, and his disciples is thus complete. The joy of each disciple is the same as the joy of Jesus, when we obey as he did. Granted, our obedience will never be perfect, and we shall often feel our wretchedness. All godly men have. But that sense of wretchedness did not lead them away from obedience but to Jesus Christ, to seek and receive from him cleansing and renewed strength unto more constant and personal obedience.

Commit your ways to him, child of God. Resolve to obey him. Begin obeying him. He will give you grace. This is the only legitimate and satisfying personal relationship with Jesus Christ – to walk as he walked (1 John 2:6), to walk with him in the path of obedience. None of the great works of God of which we read in Scripture – the children of Israel crossing the Red Sea, the three Hebrew children resisting Nebuchadnezzar's idolatrous decree – was accomplished by knowing exactly what would happen. They had to act upon God's command. We must move ahead at the command of God. His word is life. The flesh – our fallen reasoning or feelings – profits nothing.

Along the way, he will show you his "secret," his intimate love and joy (Ps. 25:14). He always reveals himself to those who love and obey him. Is this not the way of our Savior (John 15:9-

11)? Having poured out his heart to the Father in Gethsemane, he went forth to meet his accusers, thus initiating his own agony. Why would he do this? Nothing brought him more joy than obeying his Father. He obeyed his Father because love for his Father was more precious to him than his dread of the cross. He will share the same love and joy with us as we obey him (John 14:21-23). Then, filled with his joy and upheld by his loving omnipotence, we shall walk as he walked. We shall bring forth much fruit. God will be glorified. Our joy will be strengthened and move one step closer to his eternal kingdom.

The Imitation of Christ

The imitation of Christ has gripped our hearts for two millennia. This holy calling allures more strongly in times of dissatisfaction and alarm at status quo spirituality: dead orthodoxy, flagging faith, and worldliness in the church. The calling is a noble one. It is also commanded: "He that saith he abideth in him ought himself also so to walk, even as he walked" (1 John 2:6). Christ-likeness shall not be realized, however, by seeking hidden meanings and symbolism in Scripture, a more direct experience of God or the Divine, and certainly not by a giddy spirituality severed from obedience to God's word. Mystics, spiritualists, and antinomians have suggested such approaches. None has resulted in the imitation of Christ but in paradigms that push us further from our Savior and leave us thoroughly dissatisfied.

To arrive at a just definition of the imitation of Christ, we must first have clear views of his person. While every believer is called to be like his Master (Matt. 10:25), some aspects of his walk are inimitable. We cannot fast forty days and nights, raise the dead, or command the seas. As the Mediator of the covenant, the Lord Jesus was given power and authority that we do not possess. Therefore, whenever we speak of imitating him, we must bow before the majesty of the Savior of the world. He did things that we cannot. He alone enjoyed a direct, unmediated fellowship with the Father. Some of his words we can barely grasp; others leave us utterly dumbfounded. Even his enemies marked this, and it infuriated them. As his friends, we wonder and worship.

At the same time, his obedient heart and daily walk are clearly revealed for our imitation. Let us begin with his heart. He said of himself: "Then said I, Lo, I come: in the volume of the book it is written of me, I delight to do thy will, O my God: yea, thy law is within my heart" (Ps. 40:7-8). Here is the key to his holy soul and the efficacy behind his sacrifice. He loved God's law; he delighted in doing his Father's will above all else. He told his disciples: "My meat is to do the will of him that sent me, and to finish his work" (John 4:34). Any imitation of Christ on our part must begin from the same place that our Lord began. His was no mystical "I have an inner feeling" walk with God. Though he was the very Word of God, he voluntarily placed himself under his own word! He delighted in the written word as a true and sufficient revelation of God's will. For him, walking with God was obedience to the revealed will of God. Nothing was more important to him or more determinative for his entire work as our Mediator.

Imitating Christ, walking as he walked, must therefore begin with a heart held captive to God's word. Since we lost this heart in the garden, we must be born again. We cannot imitate our Savior before we are renewed by his power. Ever has the Church struggled to begin here, where the Bible does, with the new birth. Sadly, she has often substituted moralism for regeneration; sometimes mysticism and flight from the world of sense. Notice, however, that while in the world and not trying to escape from it, our Lord Jesus delighted in God's law and obeyed it with every ounce of his being. Only God can give us such a heart. He does so by taking away our heart of stone, that blind and hard heart with which we are born, and by giving us a heart of flesh, a pliable, yielding, and submissive heart that delights to obey him. The high note of supernatural regeneration must be sounded again, or else there can be no imitation of Jesus Christ. "Ye must be born again" were our Lord's first words to Nicodemus. They are the first steps to the imitation of Christ.

The failure to preach and disciple in terms of this supernatural gospel of regeneration is the most disturbing trend in the western church. Its omission, neglect, and naturalization are the death of true Christianity. Therefore, we must humbly yet boldly protest whenever moralism is substituted for regeneration. "Being good" takes many forms, from trying to be a nice and moral person to filling one's life with ostensibly Christian activity as a way to feel better about oneself. With moralism comes the tendency to "cure" the sinner's spiritual problems with counseling and "life principles." These may well clean up the periphery of his life, i.e., drug abuse, immorality, financial or family problems, but they do so without challenging the sinner's heart of rebellion. It requires no great spiritual discernment to desire recovery from the miserable consequences of sin. It requires the work of the Holy Spirit to see oneself as a sinner, to exclaim with Peter, "Depart from me, O Lord, for I am a sinful man" (Luke 5:8).

Yet, the sinner's fundamental problem is not sin's consequences but sin's guilt before a holy God and sin's horrible dominion over his life. Too much focus on the consequences of sin and helping sinners clean up their lives without confronting them with the filth of their sins and the sole remedy in Christ's blood and righteousness will make good moralists but not good disciples. "You can do it" pep rallies will only increase our pride and obscure our weakness and total dependence upon the power and mercy of God. Such false gospels will not result in the imitation of Christ but in the taming of the gospel or its replacement with decisionalism, seven steps, or addiction recovery. Against these, the sinner may be cured only by God's regenerating work. This may well be the reason that the new birth is not more commonly preached. It is not something we can control or measure. It does not make men feel good to hear that they cannot save or cure themselves. It places us solely at the mercy of God.

Preaching this gospel also lays the only legitimate foundation for the imitation of Christ. The new birth means that God restores his image in us. As Peter wrote, We are born of incorruptible seed (1 Pet. 1:23). John adds that "whosoever is born of God doth not commit sin, for his seed remains in him: and he cannot sin, because he is born of God" (1 John 3:9). This does not mean we shall be sinless, a lie John has already denounced (1 John 1:8-2:1). Rather, since God has regenerated us and implanted a new nature within us, we shall be like him. Sin shall not have dominion over us (Rom. 6:1-14). We shall be strengthened with power by the Holy Spirit to imitate our blessed Savior. The goal of our renewal is perfect Christ-likeness (1 John 3:2). He was made like unto us, his sinful brothers and sisters, to redeem us from our sins so that we might be made like unto him in holiness and joy and blessedness.

As we await his glorious appearance and our transformation, we are joined to him by the Holy Spirit. This communion of life enables us to "walk as he walked" (1 John 3:6). Thus, the imitation of Christ is not mysticism. It is also not removed from the concerns and trials of daily life but very connected to them. Was not our

Savior the Man of Sorrows? Was he not tempted in every way as we are? He had nowhere to lay his hand and was "stricken, smitten, and afflicted" (Isa. 53:4). Yet, through his humiliation, which he voluntarily undertook to redeem us, his practice was to make his prayer to the God of his life, do good to all, and to obey God with his whole heart. This was his joy (John 15:9-11). He delighted to do his Father's will. When he suffered, he "committed his soul to him that judges righteously" (1 Pet. 2:23). He will strengthen us to do the same. He will give us his Spirit if we ask (Luke 11:13), work in us mightily by his grace, and help us in our hour of need. This is the way he walked: simple yet contented, persecuted yet merciful, poor and sorrowful yet obedient and joyful, humble yet glorious.

Christian, this is the path of discipleship. It is your earthly peace and your eternal joy. "Pray without ceasing" (1 Thess. 5:18). Do as Jesus did; make your prayer to the God of your life. Never undertake anything without asking for the Father's leading, blessing, and protection. Always "set the Lord before you" (Ps. 16:8). Say: "Father, not my will, but yours be done." From this posture, there is strength to imitate Christ. Notice that after his prayer in the garden of sorrows, he rose to meet his enemies, to confound his accusers, and to triumph over the prince of darkness. When we are lowly and pray, we rise and do valiantly, in matters great and small.

Commit each day to obeying the revealed will of God. You are never more like Jesus Christ than obeying when you feel weak, forgiving when you are abused, and serving when unappreciated. Do your work heartily unto him, at intervals pausing to ask his blessing. At home, train your children to walk in his ways and show them Christ by your example of wisdom, humility, and service. Do not wait until you feel strong before you start obeying him. A godly life, like a clean house, is the result of one faithfully completed task at a time. Do not put off until later what is best done now. A godly life is also a work in progress and never completed in this life. We must always be at repenting and trusting the Lord's promise of cleansing. Seek his grace to obey. This unheralded life is the imitation of Christ. It is the only beautiful and satisfying life. It is Christ's life in us.

Seeking New Meat

In the days of his flesh, Jesus was often hungry. On one such occasion, he sent his disciples into a nearby village to buy food while he remained seated at a well on the outskirts of town. After his interchange with the Samaritan woman, the disciples returned and urged Jesus to eat. He responded, "I have meat to eat that you know not of." Had someone brought him food? He then explained, "My meat is to do the will of him that sent me, and to finish his work" (John 4:32-34).

We are saved because Jesus was wholly consecrated to the will of his Father, to obeying every jot and tittle of God's wondrous and holy law, to seeking and doing the righteousness that is the condition of fellowship with God. While the cross is the culmination of his obedience, his life was a minute-by-minute pursuit of righteousness. We should think often of the Messianic declaration in the fortieth Psalm, which is repeated in Hebrews 10:7, 9: "Lo, I come to do your will, O God." It is of inestimable importance for us that we understand this declaration.

The Son of God came to earth to obey God in place of our disobedience, to practice submission in place of our rebellion, to delight in God's law in place of our depraved loathing of it. The writer to the Hebrews immediately follows with this conclusion: "By the which will we are sanctified through the offering of the body of Jesus once for all" (v. 10). It is because Jesus Christ perfectly obeyed the will of his Father that he was able to offer himself as the worthy substitute for sinners. It is because his meat was to do the will of the Father that we are made righteous through faith in him. His righteousness is imputed to us, credited to us through faith, which is the gift of God.

Troubled consciences find rest here and only here – in the obedience of Jesus Christ. It is not by our works of righteousness that we are right with God – we have none. It is not through the right conversion experience, or being baptized, or taking the Lord's Supper. It is because Jesus' meat was to do the will of his Father that we are righteous before God. We have the "righteousness of God." If you trust in the Lord Jesus Christ, you have the righteousness of God – perfect, infallible, efficacious, unshakeable, divine righteousness. It is this righteousness that gives unassailable confidence before God's judgment seat.

Standing there, you will turn away from your own life – considered in itself it is an embarrassment, worthy of judgment, of no avail before the scrutiny of divine, holy justice. You will look for only one face, only one righteousness in that moment – that of the sinless Lamb of God. And you will be filled with boldness because in Jesus Christ you have a righteousness that suffices before the throne of God. Think often, believer, of the active obedience of Jesus Christ. It is because his meat was to do the will of his Father that his sacrifice is sufficient, his intercession efficacious, and his person able to save you to the uttermost. Place all your confidence and hope here – nowhere else. The greatest single cause of uncertainty in the believer's life, lack of assurance, spiritual impotence, and joyless experience of grace, is the failure to consider daily the perfect obedience of Jesus Christ. You must be often looking unto Jesus in his sinless perfection and complete consecration to the will of his Father. This is the sure anchor of our soul within the veil of God's presence.

This is not the only significance, however, of Jesus' declaration to the disciples. In John's gospel, he immediately draws from it a very personal and empowering application for us. His meat is our meat. This is not only true in the sense that his righteousness is our righteousness through faith and imputation but also in the sense that his ongoing work in our lives is to transform us by his Spirit so that doing and delighting in the will of God also become our meat. We often forget that one reason for Jesus' consecration to the will of the Father is that we might seek the right meat again.

Jesus was able to sacrifice his temporal needs in order to pursue a greater need. The fields were white unto harvest, and the conversion of the Samaritan woman was the first fruit in that region harvested by the mighty sickle of his word. In Christ, we too are freed from the dominion of sin to pursue righteousness. We are not left to our own resources and strength in this pursuit. We are joined to Jesus Christ in a living union sealed by the personal presence of the Holy Spirit. We have his life in us, hidden as yet, but nonetheless operative and effectual. We have new meat, new life purpose, a new power unto godliness of which the world knows absolutely nothing. It is the life of our consecrated Savior which he gives us. In communion with him, drawing from him as the living bread, water, wine, and light, we possess all that is necessary to do the will of our Father in heaven.

Lest we dismiss this as religious enthusiasm, we should look around at the rotten meat that men are voraciously consuming in their desire to find something, anything in this sterile, valueless, and pointless order created by the secularists. Entertainment, education, material prosperity, sex, and popularity – the cumulative effect of this meat is far worse than would be a worldwide outbreak of E Coli or the Bubonic Plague. It is wrecking lives and families. It has transformed our schools from institutions of learning into lifeless, dangerous, immoral halls of secularist indoctrination. But this is what happens when men eat rotten meat – when they make doing their own wills the guiding principle of life.

Praise God for his grace to us! We were eating this rotten meat, but he has delivered us by his grace and power! In his Son, he sets before us his heavenly manna, a daily feast of participation in the life and power of Jesus Christ. O, how we must eat and share this meat! The fields remain white unto harvest, and throughout them we see sick and starving men, eating the putrefying corpse of sin. To do anything about this, every believer must devote himself to seeking the new meat of Jesus Christ, of delight in the law of God, of consecration to doing the will of God, of daily communion with our heavenly manna, Jesus Christ, the very life of God.

Believer, you have been given a tremendous gift – not only righteousness and holiness through Jesus' sinless life and sacrifice but also a new life within you. Live it. Allow nothing to hinder your pursuit of the satisfying meat of doing the will of God. It is the food that will bring joy and peace to you. It is the food that will sustain you in your hard contest with the world, the flesh, and the devil. It is the food that will enable you to live by every word that comes from God's mouth rather than the rotten meat of secularism.

It is the food that will finally bring you to heaven, where you will behold the Bread of Life and the Wine of the world. Eat only this meat, child of God – for the sake of your soul and the souls of others, for the sake of the world, and for the glory of God.

Like the Master

"The disciple is not above his teacher, nor the servant above his Lord." I first gave serious consideration to these words in college, and, quite frankly, they shook me to the depths of my soul. Jesus' life, I knew, was not one of ease and comfort. If anything, he was the busiest man who ever lived. It is impossible to estimate the number of sermons he preached, the miracles he performed, or the private visits from concerned men and women that often occupied him into the wee hours of the morning. He carried the burden of the sins of the world upon his shoulders: our penalty, misery, and powerlessness. Direct, furious Satanic attack, we have every reason to believe, was not an occasional occurrence (Luke 4:13). The stark reality of the cross stood grimly before him. On his darkest earthly night, he almost expired under the weight of approaching judgment. Having born our grief, served constantly, and suffered untold agonies of body and soul, he faced the judgment of his Father, the cup of divine judgment due to us for our iniquities.

Our Savior's life, to add another level to his grief, was hardly one we could call celebrated. Yes, he had seasons of popularity. The masses loved his steadfast opposition to the established Jewish leadership, his miracles, and even his words. But the popularity ended. When he placed his all-knowing finger on the root of man's problem, the fickle masses turn upon him with a vengeance – all but a very small band. He would accept neither safe conservatism nor radical revolution. He warned against externalism, ritualism, and sacramentalism. He pointed to the heart of man as the source of evil in the world. Because he rejected a political solution to life's ultimate problem, the Jews finally rejected him. His words placed them under the same judgment as the hated Gentiles. In the midst, then, of his sufferings, he was rejected by men. The Savior of the world stood alone.

And he calls us to imitate his life of sacrifice, suffering, and opposition? We shudder. Yet he said that his disciples are not above him. We can expect no other kind of life than he led. This does not mean, of course, that the full measure of our Savior's suffering is our lot in life. His triumph over sin, Satan, and death, the progressive growth of his kingdom, and the greater kingdom works he empowers his Church to do by the power of his Spirit means that our lives will always be easier than his. God in his goodness and providence often grants us seasons of rejoicing and reprieve, victory and rest. Nevertheless, we should anticipate at least a few drops from his cup of suffering to fall upon our lives. Paul once wrote that we carry about the death of the Lord that his life may be revealed in us (2 Cor. 4:10-11).

There is another aspect of our Savior's life that bears careful attention whenever we consider being like the Master. As gut-wrenching as his life was, our Savior promised that his joy would be fulfilled in us. He was possessed by a deep and consuming joy. He also enjoyed an incredible inward sustenance and power. He once said, "I have food to eat of which you do not know. My food is to do the will of my Father and to finish his work" (John 4:32,34). He always had a kind word, a loving touch, a moment of meaningful interaction for those struggling with sin and life's problems. Somehow, joy and cross-bearing, love and suffering, comfort and burden came together in our Savior's beautiful life. This is the great challenge of Christian discipleship – combining the joy set before our Savior with enduring the cross (Heb. 12:2). We share in this intriguing, paradoxical dynamic with our Savior, and learning the way in which to bring these together is the high point and sustaining power of Christian discipleship.

Being like the Master means, first, that we establish our complete joy in doing the will of our Father in heaven. Granted, this immediately brings conflicts with sin, for we find another law in our body that fights against the new man of righteousness that delights in God's law. But God does not measure our progress in this life by unattainable perfection but by his marvelous grace. Having our Savior's joy fulfilled in us means that behind the clouds of life, the daily duties, and the periodic hardships we endure for Christ's sake, we see by faith the face of our heavenly Father smiling at us. We see his merciful and friendly face in Jesus Christ. He knows our struggles even as he knew his Son's. He knows that we carry about the treasure of the gospel of grace in

215

jars of clay, fragile vessels that await the resurrection dawn to be renewed and filled completely with the piercing rays of divine love and glory.

Knowing our Father through Jesus, we have joy. We have his food. We have eternal life. This treasure must be nurtured and expanded through daily fellowship with our Savior, allowing the word of Christ to dwell richly in us, and enjoying his fellowship through the Spirit. If we do these things, we will have joy, his joy. We will have an inner power to resist sin and walk with God humbly. This is not an esoteric spiritual principle; it is the life, the power, and the grace of our Savior unfolding in our own lives.

This joy, because it is like our Savior's, is not joy that allows us to ignore the struggles and problems of life and the warfare with sin and Satan to which we are called. We cannot escape the discipline of the cross. It is God's will to sanctify all his children through daily participation in the cross of Jesus Christ. We will be cross-bearers, or we have no part in Christ. But it is a joyful cross-bearing – a joy that remembers sin and Satan were defeated at the cross and will be defeated in life through the power of God. It is a joy that sees one's struggle with sin as an extension of Christ's victory over sin. We are fighting the same battle he fought. He won it; we will win it, progressively now and definitively later. We are seeking the goals he sought – the glory of the Father, the salvation of sinners, and the building of the Church. We have the same helps – the promises, power and presence of God.

This is being like the Master – when we see our struggles with sin, the lingering curses of this passing-away world, and the grief we bear as contributors to joy. Through them, our Father is bringing the power of redemption directly into our lives. Through them, he is conforming us to the image of his Son. Through them, on earth and in the broader cosmic battle that rages each day, our Father is defeating the powers of hell and filling the earth with the knowledge of his glory as the waters cover the seas. He did this through our Master and Lord. He is doing it through us, for we are like him, never above him, but always in him. We share in his life, his triumphs and grief, his power and joy.

You and I must bring these two together. When we seek escapist joys – discipleship without the cross, joy without responsibility, life without struggle, they will be a hollow joy. Our joy will not be like his: deep, empowering, and engrossing. It will not satisfy. We shall remain hungry and thirsty, which is the surest proof that we have not yet eaten and drunk our Savior and partaken of his life. The tears we cry will not be like Jesus': for strength to endure to the end, for submission of our will to our Father. It will not be an emptying of our own desires that we might be filled with desire for God and supreme happiness in him. They will be tears of bitterness, of lost opportunity, of the frustration of self-inflicted misery. And the sufferings we endure, if we do not spurn them altogether, will only make us angry and confused. They will hardly lead to the crown of life. Is not the failure to bring these two together – joy and cross-bearing, joy in cross-bearing, cross-bearing as joy – the ultimate reason for the weakness that occasionally afflicts us, the spiritual depression and anxiety, the spiritual drifting and dissatisfaction?

I seek a pole-star, an immoveable anchor of the soul, a light that no darkness can extinguish. I can only have it when I am like the Master. Then, let Satan roar as he may. Let temptations rage and threaten. Let the whole world continue its topsy-turvy descent into sin and judgment. I do not like these things and do not want them. I look forward to the hour when Satan is thrown into the lake of fire, when sin breathes its last breath, and when the world is ultimately renewed by the power of God through Jesus Christ. I, you, the Church, we can only reach this glorious destiny by being like the Master – by finding our joy in the Father, carrying the cross with joy and glory, and reveling in the privilege of being in and like the One who bore it all and now bears us – in his train of victory, by his power, and unto everlasting life and joy.

Light in the Darkness

"Unto the upright there arises light in the darkness" (Ps. 112:4). The godly will have their share of afflictions in this life; none is exempt. Presently, the darkness around us is deepening. The visible church lacks clarity and conviction on fundamental doctrines, practice, and methodology. Duty calls us to take action, but our hearts are cold or cowardly, uncertain or confused. Temptations abound. The daily news gives little comfort: more economic hardship, corruption and utter folly in leaders and parties, mindless violence, titillating sensuality. Though we must take care against allowing blind men's assessment of current events to color our thinking or guide our expectations – and there is not so much a media bias as media depravity – we cannot help but sense that something is terribly wrong with the society in which we live.

When God calls his people to live in such times, soberness and vigilance are our watchwords. It is easy for us to be carried along and overwhelmed by the constant stream of news, pictures, and unbelieving commentary. Better to know less and pray more than to be so swamped with information that spiritual paralysis or frenzy clouds the soul. A sense of desperation leads some citizens to take to the streets, but their activism is a very thin veil hiding their covetousness and discontent. Others would hide, "fleeing to their mountain" until the dark times pass. Entertainment, immersion in the artificial world of the internet, and simple absorption with one's own life appear attractive alternatives to mature responsibility.

We might conclude that God has given us over, to use Paul's phrase, and is allowing us to burn (Rom. 1:28). However deserved and even likely this may be, we do not know the Lord's intentions. Our reading of current events is always fallible. The strong temptation to meddle in high things must be resisted, for there are no experts when it comes to knowing the mind of the Lord (Rom. 11:34). Until the potter is finished, the clay pot has no idea what it will be, whether it will be broken and thrown away or polished and preserved.

However horrid we may think our times are, only our Lord has endured the most intense and malicious "power of darkness" (Luke 22:53). Let us follow him and see how he faced the darkness. His agony in the garden has just ended. The disciples are fitfully sleeping. Marching up the slopes, an armed band approaches, Judas near the front. He knows why they have come. Satan is about to have his hour, but, O, it is far darker than Satan can imagine even in his blackened, absolutely depraved heart. The cup of God's judgment, not Satan's wrath, stands before him. The Priest is about to offer himself and give the full measure of submission to the claims of divine justice. Torments of body, deeper torments of soul await him.

He has already lost blood, so violent was the agitation of soul he experienced as the "sorrows of death" began to descend upon him (Mark 14:34). And what a death! The most horrific deaths of all the men who have ever died are nothing in comparison. The holy and undefiled is about to become sin. He will stand before the throne of God and receive the sentence of death: condemned in the place of sinners, to receive and swallow the terrors of holiness against sin, the justice of the consuming fire. He is unhinged by the thought. How great is the darkness, the curse and misery, of all the sins of the world, the guilt and penalty about to be laid upon him!

"I am" causes the soldiers to fall back as dead men. He could walk away, passing through the midst of them (John 8:59). Is mankind worth the price of my precious blood? No, but worthiness is not at issue. What I am about to do is all of grace. My Father's will to save poor sinners and manifest the glory of his grace and love is the only worth in question, as well as the glory of his justice and wrath in the judgment of sin and sinners. Should I call down twelve legions of angels?

Angels ministered to our Lord in the days of his flesh; this is no idle question he poses to his disciples. Yes, sinners would receive their just desert – and here is the light in the darkness – but how then would the Scriptures be fulfilled (Matt. 26:54)? There is a necessity laid upon me by the word of my Father, by my own word as the Mediator of the covenant of grace in all ages to all my people, by the word of my Spirit who testified through the prophets

219

that the "Christ must suffer, and enter into his glory" (Luke 24:26). Settled determination, indescribably glorious submission, and the awful cup of divine wrath descend upon him. He allows them to lay hands upon him and lead him away.

The disciples immediately forsake him, heading off to their various dark corners to brood and weep – and hide. Satan is trembling with hideous glee as the curtain of darkness descends over him, vainly hoping to defeat in death him whom he could not overcome in life. The Sanhedrin is illegally assembling to hear a capital case at night. Our Savior heads toward the citadel of injustice, to be condemned by a higher court that they cannot see. Was there ever such darkness? The human race has faced dark nights but none like this. The only One who can save fallen man is about to be rejected and condemned. It is intent on crucifying the Lord of glory.

Can anything be expected from this act of treason against heaven but the utter destruction of the human race by fire from heaven? And yet, light in the darkness: the Scriptures must be fulfilled. Things are not as they seem. God is working out his purposes through the evil and blindness of men (Acts 2:23). Our Savior knows the Scripture. "Thy word is true from the beginning; and every one of thy righteous judgments endures forever" (Ps. 119:160). My Father has spoken; I have come to do his will. I must suffer and die, for my Father must be glorified in the salvation of my sheep, in confounding the wisdom of the world, in showing his power in my utter weakness, in pouring out love to redeem man from blindness and rebellion.

We can neither understand nor feel how deeply committed our Savior was to God's word. It guided his every step and wish. It was a part of him. It was his word as much as his Father's. As the living Word, he came to fulfill the written word spoken by his Spirit. He knew that the events of this dark night were fulfilling, must fulfill, the Scriptures. Abraham's faith must be vindicated. The promise to David's house and seed realized. Isaiah had laid out this very night's sufferings with a detail and pathos that can only be described as a prophetic miracle. It is not simply that Isaiah spoke of the sufferings of Christ; it is that the Christ spoke of his suffering through Isaiah. This is no accident. Jesus yielded himself to the power of darkness because his Father said that the salvation of sinners required it. Having determined to save us, which choice was all of mercy, no other course is open but "lay upon him the iniquity of us all," for darkness to have its final, futile hour – so that the Light of the world may dawn in all his saving fullness, power, and glory.

Let this sink into your very soul. If our Savior so revered, obeyed, and followed the Scriptures in the hour of darkness, if he viewed the Bible not so much as the writings of men but the voice of his Father, so much so that he was willing to be "numbered among the transgressors and to bare the sins of many," that same word is guiding our present darkness (Isa. 53:12). Whatever it is – personal affliction, public conflict, the deluded masses, tyrannical governments, wayward children and unloving spouses – God's word and will are being accomplished. He is clearing the rubble of darkness so that the light of our Savior's glory and kingdom may be illumined before the adoring eyes of his people and the terror-stricken gaze of the world – now and especially later. The Scriptures must be fulfilled. God must and will be glorified. Sinners must and will be saved. We must share in our Savior's suffering and weakness so that his power may rest upon us. Nothing, absolutely nothing that we experience of darkness will fail to accomplish our Father's purpose to cause light to dawn. His Scriptures alone give us this sure hope. They are the promise and path our Savior walked on that darkest night.

When we see unbelieving nations teetering – morally, philosophically, economically – are we surprised at all? The Scriptures must be fulfilled. Men and nations will either build upon the Rock that is Jesus Christ or be crushed by him. Can a man take the fire of immorality in his bosom – whether the temptress is a co-worker or an image on a computer screen – and his clothes and soul not be scorched? The Scriptures must be fulfilled. Young and old, male and female, sensuality and immorality will be cursed with broken homes, defiled souls, and societal collapse.

Can governments with God-complexes think printing presses can create value and prosperity out of thin air, and not face the judgment of God? A just weight and balance: the Scriptures must be fulfilled. There is absolutely nothing surprising or jarring about the precarious condition of the West. Nothing. The Scriptures must be fulfilled. We rejected the light of the Reformation, choosing instead the darkness of the Enlightenment. Unless we repent, we shall perish (Luke 13:3). If our Savior went to the cross in obedience to these infallible Scriptures, the Father will never allow one jot or tittle of these lines to fail to come to pass. They have been made too holy, too precious, by the sufferings and blood of the Son of God.

Shall we despair because the Scriptures are being fulfilled before our very eyes? Shall we quail in fear? Should we not instead rejoice that God is faithful to his word? Should we not speak with confidence that the darkness we are experiencing is because the men of the West are trying to hide their evil deeds (John 3:20)? Must we not testify by pity, love, holiness, and boldness that the only path of life and security lies in submission to his word? We know why current events are playing out as they are. It has little to do with the political power du jour, government education, statist hubris, easy money, easy sex, or the host of our causes that we tend to identify as the cancer at the center of our calamity. It is because we are not kissing the Son. Therefore, we are trampling upon the blood of his cross, blaspheming his name, and declaring war against the Scriptures. They must be fulfilled. Reject Christ and die. Reject the Son of God and be engulfed, slowly or suddenly, in moral, intellectual, familial, scientific, and civic darkness. His death at the decree of Scripture guarantees, certifies with his own blood, that not one word will fail to come to pass of all that God has said.

Since we know that the Scriptures must be fulfilled, we have unshakeable confidence that light will dawn for the righteousness. But we must walk in its light, as our Savior did. Since we read, for example, that our prayers ascend to heaven to be thrown back by God's hand to the earth in the form of deliverance to his people and judgment upon his enemies, shall we not pray – individually and corporately, fervently and biblically (Rev. 8:4-5)? The Scriptures must be fulfilled. God will have us seek from his hand the building of our Savior's kingdom and the establishment of righteousness on earth. Since his apostles practiced fellowship and body life as a chief way we are built up, encouraged, and motivated, shall we not give ourselves more, not less, to communion with the saints. The more evil the day, the more God's people must fellowship, meaningfully communicate with one another, engage and provoke one another to good works (Heb. 10:24). The Scriptures must be fulfilled: hover in your home, refuse to be regularly and transparently with God's people, and know only weakness. Shall we live more like the world in order to survive, be prosperous, and protect ourselves from evil times? God has made the form, the various masks, of the world obsolete. Light must not fellowship with darkness (2 Cor. 6:14-16). The Scriptures must be fulfilled.

This is our only light in the darkness. It is the path our Savior walked. It led him to the cross, to unspeakable suffering. It led him through the darkness to life, the empty tomb, and the promised glory and throne at his Father's right hand. Whatever the cost, whatever the sacrifice, we must obey God's word. It will humble us, as it did our Savior, but this is so that we may enjoy more light. An open Bible and an obedient heart will bring eternal light and life into our families. The light of God's word will give wisdom in our relationships, purpose in our daily activities, and joy in our duties. These are the old paths, but they are the paths of light. They are the paths that Jesus walked, and he was surrounded with darkness! When we are tempted and tried, let us remember that the Scriptures must be fulfilled. This is the bedrock of the universe. Against this rock, Satan and all his malice must crash and break. God will be glorified in the fulfillment of his word. He sent his Son to be the light of the world. His kingdom will grow and fill the earth. The precious blood of our Savior assures us that the word of God is our life and will give us a future of light.